Basic Christian Living

Basic Christian Living

Ian Barclay

Inter-Varsity Press

INTER-VARSITY PRESS
38 De Montfort Street, Leicester LEI 7GP, England

First published 1994
Reprinted 1995, 1999

British Library Cataloguing in Publication Data
A catalogue record for this book is available from the British Library.

ISBN 0-85110-874-1

Study guide by David Stone

Photoset in Great Britain by Parker Typesetting Service, Leicester
Printed and bound in Great Britain by Cox & Wyman Ltd, Reading, Berkshire

Inter-Varsity Press is the book-publishing division of the Universities and Colleges Christian Fellowship (formerly the Inter-Varsity Fellowship), a student movement linking Christian Unions in universities and colleges throughout the United Kingdom and the Republic of Ireland, and a member movement of the International Fellowship of Evangelical Students. For information about local and national activities write to UCCF, 38 De Montfort Street, Leicester LE1 7GP.

Contents

I

Distilled Christianity

(Ephesians 1:1–2)

At the turn of the century, a young man living in the Highlands of Scotland read Paul's letter to the Ephesians. It had such a profound effect on him that it completely changed his life. The youngster's name was John Mackay. Paul's letter so moved him that, one starlit summer evening as he sat among the rocks and crags of the Highland hills, he gave his life to Christ. Later he described what happened: 'I saw a new world . . . Everything was new . . . I had a new outlook, new experiences, new attitudes to other people. I loved God. Jesus Christ became the centre of everything . . . I had been "quickened"; I was really alive.'[1]

The young man went on to become the President of Princeton Theological Seminary. He never forgot what happened that summer evening in July 1903 and he never lost his love or fascination for Paul's Ephesian letter. Indeed, when asked to lecture at Edinburgh University in 1948, he chose Ephesians as his subject, because it was 'the distilled essence of the Christian Religion'.[2]

In *Basic Christian Living* we are going to look at this letter, because if John Mackay was right, it contains almost all that we need to know about the Christian life. The letter to the Ephesians is a course in 'Christian basics'. We can supplement our knowledge of

7

Christianity from time to time – indeed, we must if we are to grow as Christians – but we shall only be building on the foundation of the truth that we are given in Ephesians. So let's begin our study of basic Christian living. (The entire text of the letter is to be found, in the NIV translation, at the end of this book, for easy reference.)

A fairly typical letter

Paul's letter, although it contains glorious truth ('truth that sings, doctrine set to music', are John Mackay's words),[3] is also a fairly typical letter of the time. Papyrus was the substance used in the ancient world for letters and documents. It was made from tiny strips of the pith of a bulrush that grew on the banks of the Nile. These tiny strips were laid on top of each other and the result was a substance rather like brown paper. Providing it was kept free from moisture, this writing material was brittle but almost indestructible. The dry desert sands of the Middle East have proved to be an ideal place for preserving papyrus. And so archaeologists have been able to cull a wealth of documents from ancient rubbish dumps, including hundreds of private letters.

The pattern of these letters is very often the same: a greeting; a prayer for the recipients, followed by thanksgiving then the particular message of the letter; concluding with a salutation and signing off. Almost all of Paul's letters fit this pattern, and his letter to the Ephesians is no exception. So Paul's letter is quite a typical letter of his day.

The writer

The letter starts: 'Paul, an apostle . . . .' His name had originally been 'Saul' (Acts 7:58) and he was from the tribe of Benjamin (Phil. 3:5). He was probably named after the first king of Israel, who came from the same tribe (1 Sa. 9:1). But there the similarity ends, because, unlike the king, Saul of Tarsus was a rabbi who always sought to be faithful and obedient to God. When we first see Saul in the New Testament he was the leader of a zealous and misguided anti-Christian group. It was when he set out for Damascus, in an extremely violent frame of mind and bent on arresting the Christians there, that Jesus 'captured' and converted him (Acts 9:3; 28:1–32).

Saul now became Paul, the apostle to the Gentiles or non-Jews. He was worshipping with the Christians in Antioch when the Holy Spirit actually called him to this task (Acts 13:2).

Luke's record of the exploits of the early church (the Acts of the Apostles) tells of the three main journeys that Paul took across most of the Roman Empire, in what must be one of the greatest evangelistic enterprises in human history.

Paul probably went to Ephesus first in AD 53, but he didn't stay very long (Acts 18:19–21). Two years later he returned (Acts 19:1–41). On this occasion Ephesus became his base for nearly three years. He planted a church there, and carried out an intensive evangelistic campaign throughout the whole region, which included hiring the lecture hall of Tyrannus in Ephesus for two years so that he could hold daily public discussions about Christianity (Acts 19:9). In Luke's words, he made sure that 'all the Jews and the Greeks in the province . . . heard the word of Lord' (Acts 19:10).

Colosse was possibly one of the other churches planted at this time. There the believers probably met in the home of Philemon.

Some ten years after Paul's first visit to Ephesus, he was arrested by a violent mob in Jerusalem. But his Roman citizenship brought certain privileges (Acts 21:30–36), including eventually an appeal to the Emperor. He was taken to Rome (Acts 25:25; 27:1), where he wrote several letters. He was a prisoner when he wrote to the Ephesians (Eph. 3:1; 4:1); in his famous phrase, he was 'an ambassador in chains' (Eph. 6:20).

The owner of the house in Colosse, where the church met, had a slave called Onesimus who had absconded to Rome, where he came under Paul's preaching and was converted. Perhaps in AD 62, Tychicus, a pastor of the Colossian church, went to Rome to discuss church problems with Paul, and, together with Onesimus, visited Paul in prison.

It seems that Paul took advantage of the visit of these two men, and when they returned home, he used them as 'postmen' for three letters: the letters to the Ephesians, to the Colossians and to Philemon. At the same time he sent Onesimus back to his master.

A snapshot of Ephesus

People tend to feel comfortable when surrounded by familiar things. Most modern Western men and women would feel at home in Ephesus.

It was a port on the Aegean sea, situated on three overland trade routes. Caravans from the East would arrive in Ephesus with goods to be shipped on to the other parts of the Roman Empire. Many feel that John's description of Rome in Revelation evokes the sights, sounds and smells of Ephesus:

> Cargoes of gold, silver, precious stones and pearls; fine linen, purple, silk and scarlet cloth;

every sort of citron wood, and articles of every kind made of ivory, costly wood, bronze, iron and marble; cargoes of cinnamon and spice, of incense, myrrh and frankincense, of wine and olive oil, of fine flour and wheat; cattle and sheep; horses and carriages; and bodies and souls of men.

(Rev. 18:12–13)

Ephesus was also an important centre for sports. The Pan-Ionian Games, the major athletics event of the province, were held there once a year in May.

It was a salacious city with a tremendous emphasis on sex. One of the seven wonders of the ancient world was the temple of Diana in Ephesus. Diana was 'worshipped throughout the province of Asia and the world' (Acts 19:27); and the adulation of Diana took the form of licentious rites performed with the temple's many libidinous priestesses.

Perhaps surprisingly, Ephesus was already an ecological disaster area. The deforestation of the surrounding hills meant that the rain had carried the topsoil into the rivers, which was slowly causing the harbour to silt up. The extent of this calamity can be seen in the fact that Ephesus was lost for hundreds of years, and was rediscovered only in 1869 many feet below a swamp 'near a stagnant pond, loud with summer frogs'.[4] By the nineteenth century the sea was six miles away. What was once the harbour of the flourishing city is today a 'marsh dense with weeds'.[5]

There is reason to believe that the harbour was already unnavigable by Paul's day, or at least sometimes choked. This would explain why he met the elders of Ephesus at Miletus (Acts 20:17).

11

Like so many of our cities, the pomp and splendour of tradition were much in evidence. Ephesus was an 'assize town', which meant that at regular intervals the governor of the province would arrive to administer the law, accompanied by all the rich pageantry of the Roman judicial system.

The city was also held in the grip of superstition. One of Diana's many titles was *Kosmokrator* or 'World Ruler'.[6] At first there seems to have been a possibility that 'Jesus' might have become just another 'name' to add to an already powerful armoury of magic names in Ephesus. That is why Paul, when speaking of God's power in raising Jesus from the dead, said that God had seated him in heaven *above* any other rule, authority, power or dominion (Eph. 1:22). So Christians were to see Jesus as the person in authority *above* everyone and everything else.

Religious pluralism

Most societies in the world today are struggling with religious pluralism. Even in England over the past five years a new mosque has been completed every two weeks, with the result that the minaret and the parish church spire now dominate the skyline together in many urban parts of the country. While it is true that we must respect the cultural background of our neighbours, there is a tendency, as there was in Ephesus, to put all religions on a par with each other and to say that our particular choice is simply the one that we find the most helpful.

What Paul does in this letter is to recognize that there are many spiritual forces at work in the world which can dominate and have power over the lives of individual men and women, but standing head and shoulders above them all is Jesus Christ.

So we need to note that if, in the past, we've been in contact with one of the old historic religions, or a cult, or even a contemporary religious movement such as the New Age, when we come to Christ we have nothing to fear from the past. We are accepted by one who is 'far above . . . every title that can be given, not only in the present age but also in the one to come' (Eph. 1:21). The early church described Jesus as *Pantokrator* – All-powerful.

A portrait of a Christian

'Paul, an apostle . . .' (Eph. 1:1). We have already seen that it was Paul who wrote this letter. Now notice how he describes himself. He is 'an apostle'. In general terms this means someone who was 'a missionary'; someone sent out by the church, like Timothy, Silvanus or Barnabas (1 Thes. 2:6 and Acts 14:14). But it also refers historically to those who received their commission directly from Christ, such as the original twelve disciples and Paul (Luke 5:4–11 etc. and Acts 9).

'To the saints in Ephesus, the faithful in Christ Jesus' (Eph. 1:1). The way Paul addresses the Christians is a useful brief summary of what it means to be a believer.

They are 'the saints'. When this word is used today, most people think of exaggerated forms of piety, or people who are so mystical and other-worldly that they don't really fit in with today's world. But the word must be understood against its Old Testament background. In his love God had separated the people of Israel from other nations, to be his people in the world. That is exactly what it means to be a 'saint'. Saints are the people who are marked off as belonging to God *in their time and in their culture*. There is little use in being the sort of people who might appear to belong to God if they had lived in the 1890s or even the 1980s. We must be those who are obviously God's people today.

They are 'in Ephesus'. The earliest papyri and most of the early manuscripts don't have the words 'in Ephesus'. There is a gap where the words should appear. Scholars feel that this isn't because Paul didn't write to the Ephesians, but, rather, because the early church felt that the letter should have a much wider readership.[7] At the very least it should be read by the church in the whole province, if not further afield. So from the earliest times the letter to the Ephesians was regarded as containing teaching that was fundamental for the whole church. It was for 'all who love our Lord Jesus Christ with an undying love' (Eph. 6:24); for all believers, wherever they found themselves to be. It didn't matter if they were in Ephesus, Egypt or Ely; or Colosse, Carthage or Coventry. The message was to the church in every place.

They are 'the faithful'. This word has two meanings: it speaks of both the *trusting* and the *trustworthy*. We need to be both of these things. There is no point in being one and not the other. If we are trusting, looking for all that God has for us today, we must also be willing to be trustworthy, the sort of people that he can trust with all he wants to give. Equally, the reverse is true. There is no point in being trustworthy if we are not also trusting.

They are 'in Christ Jesus'. As a root goes down into the ground, as a fish swims in the water and as a bird flies in the air, so the believer is 'in Christ'. It is the Christian's natural environment; it is the place where he or she finds security. It's like being a goldfish in a glass

14

tank. It doesn't matter where you put the tank; it can be in Northern Ireland or in the White House. The fish's safety is in the tank. So the believer finds sanctuary 'in Christ'.

The opening greeting

'Grace and peace' (Eph. 1:2). We have noticed already that it was usual in the ancient world for a letter to begin with a greeting. The Greek salutation was 'Rejoice', and the Hebrew one was 'Peace'. Paul combines these two greetings and slightly changes one so that it becomes the much richer word 'Grace'. Both words are full of meaning. One writer said that 'peace' is 'not dull stagnation but is a soaring, stirring, happy thing'.[8] In the Old Testament it can mean 'victory', 'a friend', 'prosperity', 'a time of security and calm', or 'physical health' (1 Ki. 22:27; Je. 20:10; Jb. 15:21; Jdg. 6:23; Ps. 38:3). 'Grace' refers to God's sheer initiative in saving us. We are reconciled to him through his free and undeserved mercy. (Ephesians 2:6–9 will remind us of God's incomparable kindness to us in sending Jesus – we are saved by grace, not by our human efforts.) Paul wishes the fullest form of both 'Grace and peace' to be his readers' experience.

2

The A-B-C of the gospel
(Ephesians 1:3–14)

The next section of this letter (Eph. 1:3–14) is a single
sentence; Paul doesn't stop to punctuate or pause for
breath. What he has to say flows from him like a great
waterfall of cascading truth. It's like a splendid hymn
of praise, or a magnificent creed declaring all that we
can enjoy in Christ, or a marvellous benediction which
is both weighty and full of truth. It is doctrine set to
music.

There is a discernible thread running through the
passage. This is the little phrase we have already
noticed: 'in Christ'. So let's take this thread and hang
on to it some of the glorious gems of truth that Paul
informs us are ours in Christ. These truths can be
strung on the thread in alphabetical order:

A: we are *adopted* as God's children

'Adopted as his sons' (Eph. 1:5) is the way Paul puts it;
literally the Greek reads, 'placed as a son'. Adoption is
an important New Testament picture, telling us a great
deal about what we have already become in Christ and
about our status and standing as believers. This
picture does not refer to anything that we have to
achieve by ourselves. Rather, it is saying what God
'has freely given us in the One he loves'.

To understand this fully, it is helpful to notice

something about the Roman world. The whole concept of family life was based on the father's authority; he had absolute control over his children. A Roman child never came of age until his father was dead. No matter how old the child was, while his father was alive he remained firmly under his father's control. The adoption process included a lengthy legal procedure of breaking the original father's rights, or his *patria potestas*, and putting the child under the jurisdiction of the new father. Only when this protracted operation had taken place, when the legalities had been signed and sealed, was the adoption actually complete.

Once adopted, the person was fully and legitimately a member of the new family, and entitled to all benefits and rights as such. He was now an heir, and natural children born after his adoption couldn't affect this. The old life prior to adoption had completely gone. Any debts were wiped out, because he was now a member of a new family and the old life no longer existed. In the eyes of the law the adopted young man was literally the son of the new father.

As believers we have been 'adopted as [God's] sons', and all the rights and entitlements of the new family are ours. Our spiritual debts have been wiped out and the slate is clean.

A great deal is ours already; the *fact* of our adoption is real and present. But a look at other parts of the New Testament will remind us that the final stage of our adoption won't be complete until the 'redemption of our bodies' (Rom. 8:23), 'when death has been swallowed up in victory' (1 Cor. 15:54).

B: we have been *blessed* in Christ

It is not normally good for us to hear eulogies about ourselves, but that is what we are about to experience. Paul says, 'Praise be to the God and Father of our Lord Jesus Christ, who has blessed us in the heavenly realms with every spiritual blessing in Christ' (Eph. 1:3). The words 'praise', 'blessed' and 'blessing' are all the same as our word 'eulogy'. So what begins as a eulogy addressed to God becomes a eulogy of the blessings we have received.

Notice that it's not a question of where we live, or when we lived, or the education we might have had or not had. It is not even a question of whether we are good or bad Christians. We might give ourselves only two out of ten for prayer, and one out of ten for holiness. Our success as Christians is not under debate at the moment. The only question we have to ask is, '*Are we in Christ?*' If the answer is 'Yes', then we have already been blessed 'in the heavenly realms' with 'every spiritual blessing'.

The 'heavenly realms' are the place of spiritual reality for us as God's adopted sons and daughters, and not this changing world of shadows in which we live. Heaven is our real home, because as Christians we should be living as 'aliens and strangers in the world' (1 Pet. 2:11).

Although these blessings are really ours, we still have to struggle with the tension between those parts of the heavenly life which we can enjoy now and those which we'll have to wait for.

Almost all of the blessings of our life 'in Christ' which are revealed in the New Testament have a *now* aspect and a *not yet* aspect. We have been *saved*. It is true to say

19

that our redemption lacks nothing, yet it is equally true that our salvation won't be complete until we get to heaven and enjoy 'the redemption of our bodies' (Rom. 8:23). We have been *adopted*. The rights and authority of our old father, whom C. S. Lewis called 'Our Father Below',[1] have gone for ever and we are now members of a new family and can start to savour all its privileges. But our adoption won't be complete until we leave these 'shadowlands'[2] and get to heaven.

We must learn to live within the tension between the *now* and the *not yet*, while striving to possess as much as we can of the heavenly life. We have been 'blessed' with 'every spiritual blessing in Christ', but clearly we won't be able to relish 100% of these blessings until we get to heaven.

There is probably no greater contemporary dilemma facing Christians today than our inability to grasp the truth of both the *now* and the *not yet*. Not to see all that we have in Christ is to lack spiritual vision, but to expect too much now is to lack spiritual realism – and that is unhealthy. We need to be men and women of two worlds – determined to acknowledge that nothing is impossible with God, but at the same time accepting the fact that not everything is possible for us while we're still in this 'broken' world.

My wife has recently been helping a friend through a messy divorce. The friend's struggle has been to keep her eyes on all that she has and is in Christ; that is, the *now*. The *not yet* has meant that she's had to battle through the discouragement of unpleasant things being said in court, the mess of trying to divide a family home, accepting other people's view of a just financial settlement, and many other blows which have cast her down.

Again the Bible is abundantly helpful and throws light on our problem. The book of Job shows how a man in the depth of human loss and degradation can still say, 'I know that my Redeemer lives' (Jb. 19:25) – that is the *now* and the *not yet*.

C: we have been *chosen* by God

'For he chose us in him before the creation of the world . . . he predestined us' (Eph. 1:4–5). The word 'predestined' literally means 'marked out beforehand'. We've been 'earmarked' by God – that's the way one writer puts it.[3] We're earmarked by God's grace for his grace. Every believer carries this mark of God's eternal goodwill. Note that it is 'in love' that 'he predestined us'; it's not a stroke of fate, but the deliberate act of a gracious, loving Father.

God's earmarking is obviously a doctrine that can be wrongly applied and abused. This doctrine is not meant to inflate our arrogance and make us feel special in the wrong way, nor is it meant to quench the hopes and desires of those who are seeking God.

A number of Christian autobiographers, in describing their search for God, say that when they discovered him, they found that it was he who had been looking for them all along. That's what Paul is talking about here. C. S. Lewis wrote in his autobiography, 'Amiable agnostics will talk cheerfully about a man's search for God. To me . . . they might as well have talked about a mouse's search for the cat.' Then he speaks of God closing in on him.[4]

To the praise of his glorious grace' (Eph. 1:6). This is the first of three great outbursts of praise by Paul. It is one of the features of the letter that Paul wants us to know that the greatness of God's majesty is to be seen in his 'glory', 'grace' and 'power'; it is a theme that runs right through this letter.

D: we are *delivered* in Christ

'In him we have redemption through his blood' (Eph. 1:7). The older translations use the word 'deliverance' instead of 'redemption'. Strictly speaking, the Greek word means 'ransomed'. It was the word used to refer to the payment made to free a slave, a hostage, or prisoner of war. It could be used to describe the experience of a man who had been set free from the death penalty. It is also the word which the Bible uses to describe God's deliverance of his people from their slavery in Egypt.

We use the word today, if at all, when we 'redeem' trading stamps, or if we 'redeem' something from a pawnshop. In the business world documents are still 'redeemed'.

Perhaps the best way to understand redemption today is to see it as the ransom price paid to deliver those who were quite incapable of freeing themselves, such as Roman slaves. We are slaves of sin, and the ransom price paid to free us was the death of Christ; 'we have redemption through his blood'. There is no way that we could have achieved this freedom for ourselves.

E: we've been *enlightened* by Christ

He has 'lavished on us . . . all wisdom and understanding. And he made known to us the mystery of his will' (Eph. 1:8–9). When Jesus was with his disciples in Caesarea Philippi he asked them, 'Who do people say that I am?' The disciples gave a variety of answers. In the end Jesus said to Peter, 'Who do you say I am?'

Peter replied, 'You are the Christ, the Son of the living God.' Jesus said, 'This was not revealed to you by man, but by my Father in heaven' (Mt. 16:17).

The human mind is a powerful instrument. We must use our minds and develop them as much as we can. In the past men and women have used their intellects to unravel some of the secrets of the universe. But there are things that we will never be able to discover, no matter how much we exercise our minds; these are the truths pertaining to the person of God. We can know these only if God chooses to reveal them to us. The word 'mystery' in the New Testament speaks of *the truth that has been revealed*. It was a mystery, but God has now chosen to reveal it to us. 'Wisdom' is knowledge that sees to the heart of things, and 'understanding' is insight that leads to right actions and behaviour. The mystery of God's will, the secret of all wisdom and the revealing of all understanding are in Jesus Christ. We have an accessible summary of this in our Bibles. The Bible is *revealed truth* – mystery made plain. But even as we read our Bibles we still need God to enlighten our minds.

F: we are *forgiven* in Christ

'In him we have . . . the forgiveness of sins' (Eph. 1:7). At the heart of the gospel is 'forgiveness of sins'. Paul's word for 'sin' here means 'a falling by the wayside', a 'stepping aside' from the path that we should be taking. In one of the other prison letters Paul uses the Greek word which means 'missing the mark' (Col. 1:14). This is the more common New Testament word to describe our failure to conform to God's will. In English we have only one word, 'sin'. Once we 'miss the mark' or 'step aside' from the best that God expects from us, then we have become sinners. This is long before we've done anything that the world classifies as 'sin'.

It is necessary to go back to the Old Testament to understand the idea of sin fully. Essentially it is *rebellion against God*. That is why the Bible can say, 'All have sinned and fall short of the glory of God' (Rom. 3:23). This rebelliousness is the root of sin. Roots that are alive inevitably grow, blossom, flower and bear fruit. Sin is exactly the same. The Bible can say that we are all sinners because, as part of our fallen nature, we are born in a state of rebellion against God. Then, of course, the root of this weed grows, flowers and bears fruit.

There is little point in saying rather smugly that the weed of sin isn't flowering in our lives at the moment. Even if this were true (and it is not likely to be), if the root is there it will inevitably blossom and flower. That is the nature of weeds; they always grow.

Paul says that because of the death of Christ we can have 'forgiveness'. In the Old Testament this word had a special meaning. It referred to the regular remission of debts that happened every seventh year and in the year of Jubilee. Every slave in a Hebrew household would serve for six years and then be freed in the seventh. At the end of a seven-year period every creditor would also have to release his debtors; what was owed could no longer be exacted (Ex. 21:2–11; Lv. 25:39–46; Dt. 15:11–18). The word 'forgiveness' used by Paul here describes this *remission* and *liberation*. So the death of Christ has cancelled, has released, has liberated, has discharged us from any spiritual obligation resulting from our sin. In the world of the New Testament the word 'forgiveness' was regularly used

24

for the remission of taxes or exemption from taxation.[5]
No wonder Charles Wesley could write in one of his
hymns, 'No condemnation now I dread.'

This forgiveness has been given to us 'in accordance
with the riches of God's grace that he lavished on us'
(Eph. 1:7–8). 'Riches' speak of wealth and abundance;
'grace' tells us that it is all undeserved and unmerited;
'lavished' suggests that we are generously showered
with forgiveness in an unrestrained way.

There is a picture of forgiveness that we need to
rediscover today. On the Day of Atonement in Old
Testament times a goat was sacrificed to take away the
people's sins. These sins were then symbolically trans-
ferred to a second goat which was dispatched into the
wilderness, never to be seen again. As the solitary
animal disappeared into the distance, this was a
graphic picture for the people that their sins were
carried away and gone for ever.

The New Testament shows the same truth when
John the Baptist points to Jesus and says, 'Look, the
Lamb of God, who takes away the sin of the world!'
(Jn. 1:29). The tense here is the present continuous,
and it speaks of our sins being 'lifted up and carried
away'. The death of Christ acts in a present continuous
way in the life of the believer. For the believer sin has
been, is being, and will continue to be dealt with until
he or she gets to heaven. That is part of the sheer
lavishness of the riches of unmerited grace that God
has showered upon us in Jesus Christ.

I don't find any suggestion in the New Testament
that I can be perfect until I get to heaven. There is
plenty of teaching saying that I can be more nearly
perfect than I am presently. But I find that as a believer
in Christ God is dealing with the guilt of my sins until I

leave this world of shadows. John says in his first letter that 'the blood of Jesus . . . purifies us from all sin' (1 Jn. 1:7). Here also the tense is the present continuous.

G: we are *gathered* in Christ

God is working to a plan. 'His eternal purpose' is the way Paul describes it in chapter 3 of this letter. You could translate this as 'his Masterplan'. That plan is 'to bring all things in heaven and on earth together under one head, even Christ' (Eph. 1:10).

It is very easy for our hearts to sink when we watch the news on TV and see yet another *coup d'état*, or a further major crop failure in those parts of the world which are on the brink of widespread famine. But no matter how tragic and heart-rending these events are, we need to learn to look by faith behind *secular* history to see the *spiritual* account of things. Here we see God at work in a world damaged and bruised by sin, gathering his people into his eternal kingdom. This is not to say that we mustn't help in times of catastrophe, but it is to say that we must see God's 'eternal purpose' which he 'purposed in Christ, to be put into effect when times will reach their fulfilment' (Eph. 1:9–10). And we must take heart at that. Note the little phrase, 'all things'. Nothing is going to escape God's gathering in.

H: we are *hallmarked* in Christ

'Having believed, you were marked in him with a seal, the promised Holy Spirit, who is a deposit guaranteeing our inheritance' (Eph. 1:13–14). A seal was used in many ordinary ways in Paul's day. A building could be closed up and sealed, as could a grave. The secrets of some seductive lives, such as Cleopatra's, were sealed from ordinary human beings. But the seal of ownership must have been uppermost in Paul's mind here. Sacks of grain would be sealed to indicate ownership and to promise final payment. Animals were sealed or branded, or, to use our word, even earmarked. So sealing suggests an assurance of belonging.

This sealing happens to us when we *believe*. Sealing and believing are two sides of the same coin. We are sealed with God's Holy Spirit when we are 'included in Christ, when [we hear] the word of truth and respond'. It happens to all believers. There is no suggestion of two-tier Christianity whereby some might be sealed and others not. It is the same subjective experience that enables us all to say, 'Abba, Father' (Rom. 8:15); and it is a pledge, an assurance that 'guarantees our [future] inheritance'.

A prayer for the church
(Ephesians 1:15–23)

'For this reason . . .' Paul feels compelled to pray for the Christians in Asia. He has been listing the wealth of blessing that belongs to those who are 'in Christ'. It now occurs to him that all he has been talking about, he actually shares with his Gentile readers, because they also are 'in Christ'. So now he prays for them, that they too might be able to grasp the riches that are theirs.

Faith and love

Paul sees the Ephesians as true believers because they are authenticated by their 'faith' and 'love'. In some letters faith by itself is enough for Paul's commendation (Rom. 1:8), and in others, it's the trio of 'faith, hope and love' (1 Thes. 1:3; Col. 1:4–5).

The right objects for faith and love are important, especially today, when some people would urge us to have 'faith in faith' and to have a hazy, benevolent attitude to everyone in general. What causes Paul's prayer and thanksgiving is the Ephesians' objective of 'faith in the Lord Jesus Christ' and their purposeful 'love for all the saints'.

Spiritual enlightenment

Paul prays that they will understand in their 'hearts' all that Christ has done for them (Eph. 1:18). For us living in the twentieth century, the heart is the seat of the *emotions*, and not always to be trusted, unless other things are taken into consideration. But for people living in Bible times, the heart was the location of the *intelligence and will*. We could perhaps take it a step further and say that for the Ephesians, the heart was the whole 'inner man', including a person's mind, will and emotions.

Spiritual enlightenment isn't just a question of education or IQ. It is the work of the Holy Spirit, who is 'the Spirit of wisdom and revelation' (Eph. 1:17). No matter how clever we are, unless the Holy Spirit gives us understanding, our hearts will remain 'darkened' (Eph. 4:18). That is why Jesus said of some people, 'though hearing, they do not hear or understand' (Mt. 13:13).

Because of the darkened state of our minds we must keep reminding ourselves of all that we are in Christ. Some of us are all head and no heart, while others are all heart and no head. We all need to pray that the Holy Spirit will keep the right balance in our lives, so that we strive to enjoy all that we are in Christ, but at the same time knowing that the complete experience and understanding won't be ours until we get to heaven. John Stott puts it so clearly:

> Some Christians seem to do little but pray for new spiritual blessings, apparently oblivious of the fact that God has already blessed them in Christ with every spiritual blessing. Others lay such an emphasis on the undoubted truth that everything is already theirs in Christ, that they become complacent and appear to have no appetite to know or experience their spiritual privileges more deeply.[1]

We must prayerfully preserve the tension between recognizing all that we have in Christ and seeking to enjoy more and more of him each day.

The God to whom we pray

Notice that Paul refers to 'the God of our Lord Jesus Christ' (Eph. 1:17). He has already spoken of him as 'the Father of our Lord Jesus Christ' (Eph. 1:3). Now he suggests that Jesus became such a real human being that God was his God as much as ours. It follows, therefore, that it is only through Jesus that this God can be fully known and approached. Jesus, because of his humanity and deity, is the only one who has bridged the gap between God and mankind.

Next Paul describes God as 'the glorious Father' (Eph. 1:17). This seems to mean more than the English words suggest. Other translations say that he is the 'all-glorious Father', and that appears to be what Paul is saying. God is the Father of glory; he is its origin and source and King, and therefore he is the one to whom all glory belongs.

Now we can begin to look at Paul's prayer.

The gift of God's friendship

'I keep asking . . . that you may know him better' (Eph. 1:17). Many of the men and women we meet in the Bible seem to have enjoyed an intimate friendship with God. We find them walking and talking with him in a vast variety of ordinary experiences.

Paul prays that the Ephesian believers will develop their relationship with God so that they will get to 'know him better'. He wants their experiences to deepen through friendship into a richly intimate encounter. The verb 'to know' can be used in many

31

different ways. Clearly, to know God as the people did in Bible times was to have a profoundly spiritual experience. The Bible also speaks of Adam knowing his wife, Eve, who then conceived and bore a son. In this case the word refers to something exquisitely intimate that happens between a husband and a wife.

So when Paul prays that the believers' knowledge of God might grow, it must include the whole gamut of experience, from the mysterious and profound to the exquisite and intimate.

We've already noticed that this letter is addressed 'to all who love our Lord Jesus Christ' (Eph. 6:24). Paul wants the acquaintance that all believers have with God to move on from mere awareness of his presence to the mutual love and rapport of the close friend and confidante. And we must include ourselves in the prayer too. We need to get to 'know him better' as well.

Called to enjoy hope

The outcome of getting to know God better and the consequence of having 'the eyes of [our] hearts . . . enlightened' will be that we will 'know the hope to which he has called' us (Eph. 1:18).

Two things need to be noted here. Firstly, we've been 'called' by God. 'Called ones' or 'chosen ones' would be a good way to define the word 'Christian'. Paul has touched on this already: 'he chose us in him before the creation of the world' (Eph. 1:4).

Our English word 'church' comes from New Testament words that mean 'called out'. So a church is simply a group of people who, to use Peter's language, have been 'called . . . out of darkness into [God's] wonderful light' (1 Pet. 2:9).

Secondly, we have been called to enjoy 'hope'. We normally define hope as 'something that we look forward to' or 'a future expectation or desire'. However, in the Bible, hope is something that touches the believer's whole life – past, present and future. We were chosen in him before the world began (Eph. 1:4); that is our past. Then we 'heard the word of truth, the gospel of . . . salvation' (Eph. 1:13). That was when God started the process of our redemption, conforming us 'to the likeness of his Son' (Rom. 8:29); that is our present state. Sometime in the future we shall reach the ultimate conclusion of God's work, when we see him face to face and are finally like him.

Inheriting the kingdom

God's people are his inheritance, a 'possession' that he 'chose' for himself 'before the creation of the world' (Eph. 1:4). But here Paul is talking about another truth. He is saying that an aspect of the 'hope' to which God has called us is 'the riches of [a] glorious inheritance' (Eph. 1:18).

When you first read this verse, you may have wondered whether these 'riches' and the 'glorious inheritance' are being enjoyed by God, or are entrusted by him to the believer. Some commentators interpret this one way and some the other. But the clue to what Paul is saying is the parallel passage in Colossians, where he says that we must 'give thanks to the Father, who has qualified [us] to share in the inheritance of the saints in the kingdom of light' (Col. 1:12). Paul is obviously referring to an inheritance that we are to enjoy as believers.

Not many people enjoy the prospect of inheriting a kingdom. I suppose it would be true to say that Lady

Diana Spencer woke one day to such a reality. As the bride of the Prince of Wales, she immediately shared his titles, and became the Princess of Wales, the Countess of Chester, the Duchess of Cornwall, the Duchess of Rothsay, the Countess of Carrick and Baroness Renfrew. One day, because she is the wife of the heir to the throne, there will be even more prestigious titles, properties, distinctions, and ultimately a crown.

Paul's point is that as the bride of Christ (Rev. 21:2), believers share his 'unsearchable riches (Eph. 3:18); riches that are far too vast even to be catalogued, enumerated or recorded, let alone exhausted. What is more, it's not an earthly kingdom that believers are to share, but 'the kingdom of light'.

The difficulties that the royal couple are experiencing in no way destroy the illustration. Indeed, they make it more relevant, because anything that clouds our relationship with God immediately diminishes the potential of that relationship. This is not because God decides to stop giving, but because our ability to receive is hindered. As in a marriage, any cloud that we allow to come between God and us blights our whole relationship with him.

The greatness of God's power

We are told that God's 'power' is 'incomparable'; that is, it defies description. It can't be matched by any human comparison. Indeed, it is 'immeasurable' (Eph. 1:19, RSV) beyond any approximation that we might make or even try to imagine. Having said that, Paul decides that there is perhaps just one comparison that he might use, so he says, 'it is like the working of [God's] mighty strength, which he exerted in Christ when he raised him from the dead' (Eph. 1:19–20). If we want to understand something of God's power, we must bring our minds to consider that mighty demonstration of it when God commanded the forces of heaven to defy death and a locked stone tomb, and release the body of Jesus back to life.

Note the kernel of what Paul is telling us here. This 'power' is 'for us who believe' (Eph. 1:19). I have mentioned that the occult was a feature of Ephesian society. The goddess Diana was sometimes called the 'World Ruler'.[2] Those who worshipped her were quite happy to accommodate Christianity, providing the name of Jesus was no more than another name that could be used to work magic spells and incantations. This is why Paul speaks so clearly of Christ's exaltation above everything in this world and the world to come.

Christ over everything

A good number of the Ephesian Christians had previously been involved in the occult. Luke tells us: 'Many of those who believed now came and openly confessed their evil deeds. A number who had practised sorcery brought their scrolls together and burned them publicly' (Acts 19:18–19). So Paul builds up a picture of a cosmic Christ who is above all rule, authority, power and dominion. He has been placed in this exalted position by God's power. That power is similar to 'the working of his mighty strength', which God 'exerted in Christ when he raised him from the dead and seated him at his right hand in the heavenly realms' (Eph. 1:19–20).

The fact that Jesus Christ wasn't just another powerful name among a host of magic names must have been an enormous reassurance to the Ephesians. It must have encouraged them to know for certain that

35

God had 'placed all things under his feet and appointed him head over everything' (Eph. 1:22). This should encourage us too.

4

The church

(Ephesians 1:22–23)

'And God ... appointed him to be the head over everything for the church, which is his body, the fulness of him who fills everything in every way' (Eph. 1:22–23). The 'riches' that the early Christians found in Christ were so different from anything that had gone before that the New Testament writers struggled to find new ways of describing the corporate experience that would now be enjoyed.

The new communities

In the Gospels and the Acts of the Apostles there are frequent references to the 'synagogues'. These were places where God's people gathered, and it wouldn't have been difficult to take the word 'synagogue' and use it to describe the new communities of believers that came into being as Christianity spread across the world.

But Paul chose a new word, 'church', and he did so for three reasons. Firstly, the emphasis of these new assemblies wasn't merely the fact that people had gathered; rather, it was that they had been *called together* by God; they were God's chosen people. Secondly, in the Old Testament, of course, Israel was God's chosen people, but they failed to recognize the Messiah, and they often openly attacked the gatherings of the

37

believers who did. So the words 'synagogue' and 'church' were quickly used to make the distinction between the different gatherings. Increasingly the word 'synagogue' was used for the places where Jews gathered. Thirdly, the early Christians were prepared for the change of name because Jesus had said, 'On this rock I will build my church'. The new communities that came into being would consist of people, like Peter, who openly confessed that Christ was both the Christ (Messiah) and the Lord (Mt. 16:18).

The background of the word 'church'

Although it is true that in Aramaic (the everyday language spoken by Jews in New Testament times) the word *synagōgē* (a Greek word) was used to describe gatherings of God's people, there was a Greek version of the Old Testament (called the Septuagint) which regularly used the word *ekklēsia*, which we translate as 'church'. It can be found in Deuteronomy 9:10, where the two stone tablets given by God to Moses are described: 'On them were all the commandments the LORD proclaimed to you on the mountain out of the fire, on the day of the assembly (*ekklēsia*).' This same word was used by Jesus. So it is possible to say that the word 'church' has an Old Testament background.

There is also a cultural background reflected in this Greek word *ekklēsia*. In the great Greek democracies it meant 'the ruling body', which was a group consisting of all the citizens, who together appointed magistrates and sent out ambassadors. For the people who came from such a background, 'church' spoke of the 'glories of citizenship'.[1] And so new converts familiar with such a concept would immediately think of themselves as 'citizens of the kingdom of heaven'.

Nowhere in the New Testament does the word 'church' refer to a building. It always refers to the company of worshipping people who have given their hearts and pledged their lives to Jesus Christ; to those who have been called out by God to enjoy the riches in Christ. The early church simply wouldn't understand us today when we describe going through the countryside and seeing a beautiful church.

Paul's use of the word 'church'

Paul uses it to mean *a collection of local Christians*. It is his word to describe the believers living in any particular place. So we have 'the church in Cenchrea', 'the church of the Laodiceans', and 'the churches in Galatia' (Rom. 16:1; Col. 4:16; Gal. 1:2). He called those who took gifts of money to the poor Christians in Jerusalem the 'representatives of the churches' (2 Cor. 8:23); he urged the Corinthians to show 'the proof of [their] love . . . so that all the churches [could] see it' (2 Cor. 8:24). He himself had a 'concern for all the churches' (2 Cor. 11:28). In this sense, if Paul were writing today, he would talk about the Christians in Glasgow, Taunton, or Chester.

Paul also uses the word 'church' to describe *a meeting of believers* in the way that we talk about 'congregations'. He says those with a prophetic gift are to 'edify' the church (1 Cor. 14:4). He refers to a 'whole church coming together' (verse 23). In a contemporary sense Paul would be talking about the Tron in Glasgow, St James in Taunton, or Holy Trinity in Chester.

Finally, Paul uses 'church' to describe *the universal church*. By this he means the whole company of believers in every place, every nation and every time. Paul, before he became a believer, was a persecutor of this church (Phil. 3:6). The manifold wisdom of God is shown through this church (Eph. 3:10). Glory is given to God by it (Eph. 3:21). The whole of this church is subject to Christ (Eph. 5:24); and Christ loves the whole church (Eph. 5:25). And it is this meaning of the word 'church' that is by far the most common in this letter.

Jesus the Supreme Head

Paul says that God has placed 'all things' under the feet of Christ. He has authority over everything, both in this world, where he is the 'ruler of the kings of the earth' (Rev. 1:5), and in the unseen world of spirits and demons, where he is 'Head over every power and authority' (Col. 2:10). So 'all authority in heaven and earth' is his (Mt. 28:18).

In a sense, nothing more needs to be said, but Paul takes what he wants to say a step further by pointing out that God has appointed Jesus 'head over every-thing for the church' (Eph. 1:22). Paul is underlining the fact that Jesus is the Supreme Head of the church, and the vital unifying life-force that runs through it. To us this is saying that if we have been accepted by Christ, there is nothing to fear. Anything we might fear is subject to his leadership; there are no dark spirits in the unseen world who are not under the authority of Jesus. If we are in Christ, nothing can harm us, because Jesus can and does deliver us from such things in the unseen world. He is the *Saviour* and *Deliverer* of the church. But Paul would also emphasize that part of the 'crown rights' of Jesus, as the Sovereign over all, is that he expects our obedience and our acceptance of his lordship.

The body of Christ

The idea of the church as 'the body of Christ' is unique to Paul. It is not clear what gave him the idea, but what he is saying and implying is transparently obvious. Christ and the church are a single living organism. All believers are integrally linked both to Christ and to each other in a single living whole.

In earlier letters, Paul had used the idea of the body to show that harmony can exist among Christians who are different from each other in precisely the same way that the different parts of a body function together. His argument is that a church can consist of a group of believers who, though very different from each other, are in the end mutually compatible. So in the earlier picture we see individual believers as the head (1 Cor. 12:21), and even part of the head (verse 16), just as they are all the other parts of the body too (verses 14–26).

Now, however, in Ephesians and Colossians, Paul shows Christ as the head. He is the one from whom all the other parts of the body derive their life and power. Paul has already spoken of this life and power in the resurrection of Jesus. We've seen that God, by 'the working of his mighty strength', has 'raised [Jesus] from the dead and seated him at his right hand in the heavenly realms' (Eph. 1:20). Here Paul's argument is 'as with the head so with the body', because they are intrinsically and dynamically one. He now wants to develop this argument.

The church is the 'fulness' of Christ

The word 'fulness' in the New Testament has a wide range of meanings. The common thread running through most of them is that the word is used in an active sense; in other words, something that fills. In Matthew Jesus speaks of a 'patch' that fills up a tear and makes the garment whole again (Mt. 9:16). After the feeding of the five thousand Mark says that 'the disciples picked up twelve basketfuls of broken pieces of bread and fish' (Mk. 6:43). Paul uses this word to translate a psalm: 'The earth is the Lord's, and *everything* in it' (1 Cor. 10:26), and he tells us that 'in Christ all the *fulness* of the Deity lives in bodily form' (Col. 2:9).

Outside the New Testament, in ancient times the word 'fulness' could mean the crew of a ship, and indeed today it is used in modern Greek for the crew of an airliner.

It would be easy to take Paul's previous idea that Christ is the head and to develop it along the lines of a person's head filling his body with thoughts and actions, and then to say that in a similar way the church is filled with Christ. Indeed, that is what Paul does say in another letter: 'You have been given fulness in Christ' (Col. 2:10). But here in Ephesians he is not saying that. Paul is using the word 'fulness' in a passive way to speak of the body being 'the fulness of him'. That is something quite different. God has made Christ the head of the body, and the body 'fills and completes' him. However, Christ still waits for his 'completeness', because he won't be 'complete' until the church is perfectly restored to him and he to the church. That presumably won't happen until time ends and heaven begins. One great writer in the past said:

This is the highest honour for the church, that, until he is united to us, the Son of God reckons himself in some measure imperfect. What a consolation it is for us to learn, that, not until we are with him, does he possess all his parts, or wish to be regarded as complete.[2]

The church is not as it should be

The church has been likened to a great equestrian statue with massive muscle and life-like vigour, preparing to take a mighty leap forward. But come back twenty years later and you find it on exactly the same spot. Sadly, that is the state of the church: it apparently has massive potential, but it never moves. Its life-like features seem to be inextricably set in bronze.

How we enable the church to become what it should be is really the problem that Christians have had to face in every age; and we must face it in ours.

What we can do is to make certain that, in the particular part of the body (the church) where we worship, we give the head (Jesus Christ) all that is his by right. In practical terms this means that we should obey him and submit to his rule; we have already seen that part of the 'crown rights' of his lordship is our obedience.

One of the diseases that can blight the human body is cancer. In very simple terms, cancer could be described as anarchy among the cells. The body of Christ can be similarly diseased. To end the anarchy in the part of the church where we worship, we ourselves must submit to Christ in obedience. We can also start to pray for our fellow church members, that they too will truly own him as Saviour and Lord. If we do this, the potential of the church will be realized at last, and our local community and our world will be changed as Jesus lives through his body.

5

The crooked timbers of humanity

(Ephesians 2:1–3)

In the first chapter of his letter, Paul shows God's original idea for the church: it was to be made up of people who had begun to enjoy 'every spiritual blessing in Christ' (Eph. 1:3). In a single Greek sentence he declares the great variety of spiritual richness which the Ephesians could now expect (verses 3–14). He then prays for them, that they might begin to delight in all these blessings that God has given. He prays that they will get 'to know [God] better' (verse 17); that they will begin to relish the 'glorious inheritance' of the saints (verse 18); that they will learn to appreciate the 'great power' that is now theirs (verse 19). He concludes the chapter with a picture of Christ and the church being so integrally bound together that they are a single living organism: the church is 'his body' and he is its 'head' (verses 22–23).

The question we need to ask now is 'Where did God get the basic material to start making this church?' This is precisely what Paul is about to reveal. Indeed, he takes us through the whole process, beginning with the most unpromising material and ending with a church that shares the exaltation of Christ in the 'heavenlies' (Eph. 2:6).

Sin is death

'As for you, you were dead . . .' (Eph. 2:1). A person's position outside Christ is quite desperate: he or she is 'dead'. Obviously Paul is not talking about our physical condition, but about our *moral and spiritual state*. There is always a tendency to think that it isn't as serious as it actually is, to imagine that all we're suffering from is a little bout of a 'sickness' called 'sin', and that given time we will get better. We may think that we were born with a bias that makes us drift a little off course; but that if we pull ourselves together and make an effort, we can get back on track and arrive at our destination safely. But in reality, we can't do either of these things, because morally and spiritually we are *lifeless*; we are *dead*.

In the previous chapter Paul referred to Christ being dead after the crucifixion (Eph. 1:20). His situation seemed equally impossible, but God raised him from the dead and brought him back to life. Paul will now show that the same can happen to us.

The reason for our deadness is our 'transgressions and sins' (Eph. 2:1). These two words are comprehensive and include all the inward attitudes that result in the great variety of actions which are morally wrong.

After a meeting a little while ago a lady said to me, 'I shouldn't think people today have the money or the time to sin.' I tried to explain that essentially *sin* is rebellion against God, and all the consequent actions that take place in our lives are *sins*. Society, however, may regard only some of these actions as sins. As we have already said, sin, at the root, is rebellion against God; and so the Bible says that 'all have sinned' (Rom. 3:23). And if the root is there, it will inevitably flower, blossom and bear fruit.

A walking death

'You were dead in your transgressions and sins, in which you used to live . . .' (Eph. 2:1–2). The words Paul actually uses are, 'in which you used to *walk*'. It is an expression that he will use eight times in this letter to describe different ways of living. In Ephesians 2:2–3 he defines the three areas that marked the Ephesians' old way of life before they became Christians and began Christian living; it is these that add up to a *walking death*.

Firstly, they 'followed the ways of this world' (Eph. 2:2). Before they experienced Christ, the Ephesians were like everybody else and followed 'this present evil age'. Their hopes and dreams were controlled by all that this world has to offer. It is not too difficult today to see people still controlled in this way: people whose aims, ambitions and aspirations are influenced by the soap-opera world of TV, or by what their neighbours think and have and do. It is the world swayed by the glamour of the showbusiness personality, by the ideals of the jet set or the yuppie or the weekend colour supplement. Christians, of course, still live in this world, but it has ceased to be their controlling influence. Their influence now *should be* the world which is yet to come, the kingdom of Jesus Christ.

Secondly, the Ephesians had been influenced by 'the ruler of the kingdom of the air' (Eph. 2:2). Paul is not talking about the clear air of the upper atmosphere, but the dark, dingy air that surrounds 'this dark world' (Eph. 6:12), where the evil one, 'the god of this world' (2 Cor. 4:4), is the controlling influence.

In our society we see people captivated by evil, but they are not necessarily those whom society would call evil. They are often the trendsetters whom millions of people admire and seek to emulate.

In an article about the rock singer and actor Sting, who played the role of the devil in *Brimstone and Treacle*, a newspaper said recently, 'Sting's choice of roles shows a fascination for the demonic.' In one scene he had his fans recoiling in horror as he raped a beautiful young woman who was disabled. He was clearly proud of the role and said:

> I loved making that movie. But I think people misunderstand me starring in it ... they go and see it and say, 'What a horrible movie.' But I'm glad I made it. I'm proud of it. The character was intrinsic to me ... I'm much more interested in the complex character of the villain than the upright two-dimensional hero. I'm always fascinated by the evil kind of character.[1]

The Ephesians were once like that. Like all Christians, they 'were once darkness', but now they are 'light' (Eph. 5:8). Paul's ministry had been to turn them 'from darkness to light, from the power of Satan to God' (Acts 26:17).

It is always difficult to translate accurately from one language to another, because words mean different things in different languages. You will have noticed that the New Testament speaks of Christ's death 'destroying' Satan, our 'old self' and death (Heb. 2:14; Rom. 6:6; 2 Tim. 1:10). In English we often use the word 'destroy' in a way that means 'to get rid of completely'. So if I say, 'I have destroyed my notes on Ephesians', most people would understand that I'd got rid of them and didn't expect to see them again.

But in the language of the New Testament, 'destroy' means 'to render ineffective or inactive'. That is obviously Paul's meaning here. Our old selves are still very much in evidence and, although we have eternal life in Christ, they will continue to be so until we experience physical death – unless Christ returns before we die. Similarly, it must be true of Satan, 'the ruler of the kingdom of the air', that he still exists and is very much in evidence, but he has been *rendered ineffective*.

We need to recognize this, because, being the Great Deceiver, he would like us to think otherwise. He still tries to hold us firmly under his rule, so we constantly need to affirm the truth that 'the one who is in [us] is greater than the one who is in the world' (1 Jn. 4:4).

The evil one has been defeated; he is in his death throes. On the cross Jesus rendered him ineffective (Heb. 2:14). This means that it is possible to stand up to him and not fall. Prayerfully we need to learn to do this as we depend on the Saviour's 'incomparably great power for us who believe' (Eph. 1:19).

We need to think about this, because it is a very important truth. We, like the Ephesians, live in 'this dark world' (Eph. 6:12), the place where the evil one has a controlling influence, but he has been rendered ineffective. This means that no matter how pressing his temptations, or how urgent he makes the lusts of the body, or how depraved he makes the desires of the mind, there is victory in Christ, because 'the one who is in [us] is greater than the one who is in the world' (1 Jn. 4:4).

The third area that marked the Ephesians' old way of life was that they sought to gratify 'the cravings' of their sinful nature ... following its desires and thoughts' ((Eph. 2:3).

Obviously, most if not all of the ordinary desires that are common to the human race were originally good. They were inbuilt mechanisms to regulate life. If we didn't ever crave food or desire rest, we would not live for long. Quite possibly, without sexual desire, procreation would cease and the demise of the human race would quickly follow.

But Paul is not talking about these desires being used as originally intended. Rather, he sees that when people are still under the domination of the evil one or among the 'disobedient' (Eph. 2:2), as he puts it, everything is turned upside down, and what should be a servant quickly becomes the master. Paul knows that we will understand what he is saying, because 'All of us also lived [like this] at one time' (Eph. 2:3).

The desires of the mind

It is fairly easy to recognize when an ordinary desire for food turns into galloping gluttony. Lust and sloth are not too difficult to spot either, so notice that Paul says that the 'cravings of our sinful nature' involve both 'desires and thoughts' (Eph. 2:3). Perhaps a look at another translation will make clear what Paul is saying: the RSV says we used to follow 'the desires of body and mind'.

The desires of the mind can be just as fanciful and sinful as those of the body. We need to be as vigilant about guarding our minds from exotic, absurd and excessive thoughts as we are about guarding our bodies from the temptations to which they are prone. I am becoming convinced that many of us Christians strenuously guard our bodies while leaving our minds open to the most irrational suggestions that the evil one may care to put in them.

There is a telling story of the deceitfulness of the human mind and the lust of the flesh in the life of Malcolm Muggeridge. As a young man he went to India. He hadn't entirely abandoned the idea of ordination, and for a while the topic of celibacy dominated his letters home. It would appear that two sorts of people are attracted to celibacy: those for whom sex is, for reasons of temperament or incapacity, an unimportant aspect of life, and those for whom it is such a relentless force that celibacy appears to offer the best hope of maintaining balance and even sanity. Malcolm Muggeridge belonged to this last group.

In one letter home to his father, he describes his reaction on the unexpected discovery of a woman bathing, while he was out swimming:

> She came to the river and took off her clothes and stood naked; her brown body just caught the sun. I suddenly went mad. There came to me that dryness in the back of my throat; that feeling of cruelty and strength and wild unreasonableness which is called passion. I darted with all the force of swimming I had to where she was, and then nearly fainted, for she was old and hideous and her feet were deformed and turned inwards and her skin was wrinkled and, worst of all, she was a leper. You have never seen a leper I suppose; until you have seen one, you do not know the worst that human ugliness can be. This creature grinned at me, showing a toothless mask, and the next thing I knew was that I was

swimming along in my old way in the middle of the stream – yet trembling . . .

It was the kind of lesson I needed. When I think of lust now I think of this lecherous woman. Oh, if only I could paint, I'd make a wonderful picture of a passionate boy running after her and call it: 'The lusts of the flesh.'[2]

Dead in transgressions and sins

It is sometimes difficult to come to terms with the idea that outside Christ everyone is 'dead' in their 'transgressions and sins' (Eph. 2:1). Perhaps the easiest moment to recognize it is when we are in the company of other Christians, and together we are rejoicing because of all that God has done for us. But there is no doubt that the idea is most difficult to accept when we are at home with our family, and they, although very loving and kind, don't want anything to do with our Lord and Saviour.

I wonder if you have ever noticed in the Gospels that when Jesus was on this earth he brought three very different people back to life again.

Firstly, there was the twelve-year-old daughter of Jairus, one of the rulers of the synagogue (Mt. 5:22–43). They laughed at Jesus when he suggested that she was merely 'asleep' (verse 39). But that might be a clue as to how she appeared to the people who had come to mourn her death. In death children can look warm, beautiful and attractive. But Jairus' daughter was dead, and she needed Jesus to restore her to life.

Some people who are spiritually dead are warm and attractive, but because they are outside Christ they are dead. They need Christ to restore them; nothing else will do.

Secondly, there was the son of the widow who lived in Nain (Lk. 7:11–17). His funeral was actually taking place when Jesus arrived in the little Galilean town that nestles below Mount Tabor. The pall-bearers had to stop for a moment while Jesus touched the open bier. And on that unhappy day, if we had been allowed to look into what the translators rather ana-chronistically call the 'coffin', we would have seen a corpse.

Some people outside Christ are like that; they are corpse-like, and hardly a flicker of life seems to disturb the dreariness of their existence. We see them every day: lifeless, gloomy, going about life like a cadaver and so often blind to the breath-taking events of life taking place around them. Yet, as we know, it is only by 'listening to his voice' that 'new life the dead receive'. It is only Christ who can make 'the mournful, broken hearts rejoice' and 'the humble poor believe'.[3]

Finally, very near to the time of his own death, Jesus restored Lazarus to life (Jn. 11:1). His funeral had taken place days earlier. The family, still in a state of mourning, were worried when Jesus began to talk about bringing Lazarus back to life, because they were aware that the corruption of the flesh must already have started to take place.

Some people outside Christ are like that. They are 'rotten', and we are even tempted to use the word that the old translations use about Lazarus, and to say that their lives 'stink'; moral corruption has clearly set in. Yet we know that Christ can redeem and change them, because he has done that for us.

So the 'walking dead' outside Christ can fill the whole spectrum of human life, from those whom we find warm and attractive through to the lifeless, and finally to the rotten and the morally corrupt. The truly amazing thing is that those who were dead in their 'transgressions and sins' can receive 'every spiritual blessing in Christ' (Eph. 1:3). That, in itself, must be a miracle.

God's wrath

Now let's begin to approach Paul's thinking about God's wrath. He sees that those who are 'disobedient' (those outside Christ) are 'by nature objects of wrath' (Eph. 2:2–3).

Imagine staying somewhere in the heart of the country and getting up in the middle of the night for a drink of water. You make your way down to the kitchen and put on the light. The light immediately expels the darkness, because light and darkness are mutually exclusive. We might say, 'If only the light could learn to love the darkness – then perhaps they could exist together.' It is not a question of love – by their very nature one excludes the other.

In the same way, a holy God and sinful people can't exist together. As with light and darkness, the two are mutually exclusive. In order to remove the problem, either God must change, or a person must change.

God cannot change, because he is immutable; so people must change. That essentially is what the gospel is all about. God has redeemed mankind; he has changed us. If we will humble ourselves and accept God's way of redemption, when history comes to an end, both we (now redeemed) and the holy God will exist happily together.

On being 'Eastered' by God

(Ephesians 2:4–10)

'But because of his great love for us, God, who is rich in mercy, made us alive with Christ even when we were dead in transgressions' (Eph. 2:4–5).

The terrible picture of humanity's plight is removed by the tiny word *'But'*. Paul has told us that the human race is lost in the muck and mire of sin, but *now* God has intervened and everything has changed. We were 'dead in transgressions and sins', but now, if we are 'in Christ', we have been 'saved'. Our situation has been totally and irrevocably changed by the death of Christ.

What has caused such a radical change? Why, when we were lost in the dark grave of sin, did God suddenly come to help us? Paul lists four aspects of the divine nature that are fundamental to any understanding of the God of the Bible.

God is merciful

Firstly, God is merciful. Indeed, Paul tells us that he is 'rich in mercy' (Eph. 2:4). Mercy is the great foundational truth that we find on almost every page of the Bible.

In the Old Testament, we see that people's love for God is uncertain and brief, while God's 'loving kindness', his mercy to us, is fixed and everlasting. In the New Testament his mercy includes compassion, gentleness, pity and forbearance.

God is loving

Secondly, God is loving. Paul speaks of God's 'great love for us' (Eph. 2:4). Love is the personal outworking of mercy. God saw our situation; he saw that without Christ we were dead, and came to our rescue. Love is mercy in action. The result of this 'great love' and 'rich . . . mercy' is that he has 'made us alive with Christ' (Eph. 2:5).

God is gracious

Thirdly, God is gracious. Indeed, he shows us 'the incomparable riches of his grace' (Eph. 2:7). The essence of grace is that God is on our side. He is committed to us – we, who were against him.

Moreover, the grace that God shows us is not a general attitude that he assumes towards the human race as a whole. In Christ, the grace of God is focused specifically and individually on each one of us. Grace in the New Testament is associated with Jesus Christ. He became a man in order to show us God's grace. Indeed, so much about him shows God's grace that we can say that 'grace' means 'Jesus Christ' and 'Jesus Christ' means 'grace'.

For us grace is free; God was under no obligation to give us anything. For God, grace was very costly, because it involved his Son becoming a man and voluntarily dying in our place. Grace means that all 'the incomparable riches' of God are freely showered on us – we, who deserved only death because of our transgressions and sins.

God is kind

Fourthly, God is kind. Paul speaks of God's grace

being 'expressed in his kindness' (Eph. 2:7). 'Kindness' tells of the goodness and generosity of God. In Matthew's Gospel Jesus invites those who are 'weary and burdened' to come to him, and he promises not only to give them 'rest', but also that they will find his yoke 'easy' (Mt. 11:28–30). The word 'easy' is the same as the word 'kind'; so our God is the very opposite of being fractious or irritable. Those who follow him find that he is easy and kind to serve.

Supremely we enjoy the kindness of God when we come to him for salvation, but we can also experience it in every other area of life as well. We've noticed one use of the word 'kind' by Jesus. Let's stay with this, and see the kindness of God in terms of our work and service for him.

One of the older writers has an imaginative yet powerful way of looking at the words, 'My yoke is easy and my burden is light' (Mt. 11:30). He says:

> Imagine a wise old ox, standing patiently beside the shafts of a plough. And an unbroken, stubborn young animal is about to have its first lesson in service. With increasing indignation, the foolish young ox looks at the plough, and says, 'Never!' Then, after a few moments he adds, 'If the farmer thinks I am going to do his dirty work, he's wrong! I was made to roam and graze in the wide open spaces, not to be harnessed to a plough. If he tries to hitch me to that contraption, I'll kick it into the next field.'
>
> The older, wiser ox says, 'Don't be so silly. The master's way is best for all of us. If you got your own way, grazing in the fields all

day, you'd quickly end up on the dinner table. Nothing attracts the butcher more than a well-fed body. But if you'd learn to understand, you'd see that work is good for everyone, including the master. He knows when you put your best into his work, and when he sees you doing that, he'll treat you like a king.'

The old ox says, 'If you want to learn I'll show you how to pull the plough. If you get tired don't worry, I'm next to you and I'll take the heavy share of the work.'

Jesus, with a radiant smile on His face, took the place of the wise old ox, and looking at His inexperienced, immature disciples, invited them to share His yoke.[1]

Salvation

Because of his mercy, love, grace and kindness, God has saved us. Everything that God does for us is summed up in the word *salvation*. It is probably the most comprehensive word in the Bible.

Paul so wants us to understand what it means that he actually invents three words to help us. He says that God has 'made us alive with Christ' (Eph. 2:5), 'raised us up with Christ' (verse 6), and 'seated us with him' (verse 6) in the heavenly realms. In the Greek text these phrases are in fact three specially coined words, saying in effect: we have been 'made-alive-together-with (Christ)', 'raised-together-with (Christ)' and 'seated-together-with (him)' in the heavenly world.

Imagine that Paul comes to see if we have understood all that he has been saying in this letter. The first question he asks is, 'Where are you if you are *outside* Christ?'

We don't have any difficulty with that, so we say, 'Dead in our transgressions and sins.'

'Excellent,' says Paul. 'Now, where are you *in* Christ?'

We respond, 'Sitting here reading this book.'

The expression on Paul's face shows that this wasn't the answer he expected. So he says, 'Let me put it another way. What has happened to Christ *since he died*?'

We find this a little easier, so we say, 'On the first Easter Day Christ was resurrected. A little while after that the ascension took place, and now he's seated at God's right hand in heaven.'

'Good,' says Paul. 'So *outside* Christ, you were dead in your transgressions and sins, and *in him* you are …?'

'Ah!' we say. 'We're beginning to understand what you're getting at. If we are *in Christ*, then the things that have happened to him have happened to us too?'

'Exactly,' says Paul. 'That is the essence of salvation. You've been "made-alive-together-with Christ", "raised-together-with Christ" and "seated-together-with Christ" in heaven. To put it in theological terms, "resurrection", "ascension" and "session" have begun to take place.'

John Stott remarks,

> What excites our amazement is that Paul is not talking about Christ but *about us*. Moreover, this talk about the solidarity with Christ in his resurrection and exaltation is not a piece of meaningless Christian mysticism. It bears witness to a living experience, that Christ has given us on the one hand a new life (with a sensitive awareness of the reality of God, and a

love for him and for his people) and on the other a new victory (with evil increasingly under our feet). We were dead, but have been made spiritually alive and alert. We were in captivity, but have been enthroned.[2]

'Eastered' by God

What Paul is touching on here, the poet Gerard Manley Hopkins described as letting 'God easter in us'. That's a good phrase, because it runs parallel to all that we are told by John in his Gospel. John says that if we believe in Christ (i.e. put our trust in him), we have 'eternal life' (Jn. 3:16), and that means 'the life of the age to come', which is 'resurrection life'.[3] So Paul and John were thinking along similar lines when they talked about salvation.

Paul emphasizes the fact that God has done everything to achieve salvation for us and that he gives it to us as a gift. To make the point, he piles up phrase after phrase. Salvation 'by grace', 'not from yourselves', 'not by works'; so 'no-one can boast' because 'it is the gift of God' (Eph. 2:8–9). All we have to do is to exercise 'faith'; in other words, we must put our trust in him.

We are visual aids

One reason why we are left in this 'dark world' of sin (Eph. 6:12) after we have been saved is that we are 'God's workmanship, created ... to do good works, which God prepared in advance for us to do' (Eph. 2:10). The word 'workmanship' is our word 'poem'. We are a piece of spiritual 'poetry'; one of God's works of art, a masterpiece that he has left here to show a fallen world what his kingdom is like. Earlier in the chapter Paul has put it another way, but just as power-fully. He says, God 'raised us up with Christ . . . in order that in the coming ages he might show the incomparable riches of his grace' (Eph. 2:6–7). The word 'show' would perhaps be better translated 'display'. We are meant to be an advertisement, a visual aid, even an exhibition of all that the grace of God can do in human beings.

On a day off not too long ago, my wife suggested that we might go to the Royal Academy to see an exhibition of Marc Chagall, the Russian-born artist. We caught a train to London, then a tube to Piccadilly Circus and walked to Burlington House.

Still stunned by the paintings as we left the exhibition, Hazel seemed determined to walk the long way back to the tube – was it because the sun was shining, I wondered? After we'd gone a few yards, it dawned on me that I was being taken shopping. Well, at least I had the feeling that my wallet and credit cards were. There can be few places in the world more frightening for a penurious shopper than London's West End. In Piccadilly, Regent Street and Oxford Street things seem to leap from the windows saying, 'Buy me!' As shop windows are the retailer's showcase, so we too 'show the incomparable riches' of God's grace. We are to display all that it means to be 'Eastered' by God.

The Gentiles are made heirs of God

(Ephesians 2:11–22)

If the plight of the Jews was precarious – sharing as they did in humanity's plight – then that of the Gentiles was much worse. After all, the Jews were God's people and could expect him to provide a Saviour one day (Je. 14:8). But there was no such help available for the Gentiles; to use Paul's phrase, they were 'without God', and therefore 'without hope' (Eph. 2:12).

Indeed, we can see from these verses that we Gentiles were Christless, stateless, friendless, hopeless and godless. The fact that we were 'separate from Christ' (verse 12) meant that nothing, absolutely nothing, could be done to help us. There was no-one to bring relief and no possible rescuer in sight. The 'But now' of verse 13 changes all that.

What Christ has done

Jesus destroyed the division between Jew and Gentile. The line of demarcation between the two was taken away, enabling those of us who were 'far away' to be 'brought near' and to enjoy the fulness of God's blessing.

It was Isaiah who said, 'Peace, peace, to those far and near' (Is. 57:19), and Paul sees Jesus fulfilling this prophecy; 'For he himself is our peace' (Eph. 2:14). Human beings are walking civil wars, and twentieth-century people fill their lives with constant sounds and activity to quell their restlessness. But it is all to no avail because there is no help for them, except through Christ. For it is only in Christ that we can have peace; peace with God, peace with each other, and peace with ourselves.

The world around is festering with feuds and the only possible reconciler is Christ. No class distinction, no colour bar, no Iron Curtain or Berlin Wall divided people so absolutely as the gap that existed between Jew and Gentile in the ancient world. There was an actual 'barrier', a 'dividing wall' (Eph. 2:14), across the Court of the Gentiles in the Temple at Jerusalem.[1] It carried the inscription, 'No man of another nation to enter within the fence and enclosure around the Temple. And whosoever is caught will have himself to blame that his death ensues.'[2] Jesus 'has destroyed the barrier' and 'made the two [groups of people] one' (Eph. 2:14). 'His purpose was to create in himself one new man out of the two, thus making peace, and in this one body to reconcile both of them to God through the cross' (Eph. 2:15–16).

So Jesus, who *is* peace, also becomes the *messenger* of peace. The reconciler becomes the one in whom reconciliation can be found, and so all that Isaiah prophesied is fulfilled.

Through Jesus Christ both Jew and Gentile 'have access to the Father' (Eph. 2:18). The word for a 'chamberlain' in the ancient oriental court is behind the word 'access'. The chamberlain was the person who had the task of introducing visitors into the presence of the king or emperor. But unlike the court functionary, Jesus doesn't simply open the door, announce our names and disappear. He is also 'the door' and 'the way' (Jn. 10:7; 14:6), so we are not left alone but are conducted right into the presence of the Father, the absolute God.

The privileges of this 'new man'

We are now *alive*, when we were *dead*; there is now *peace* where there was *war* and *rebellion* against God, and we who were godless can now enter God's presence because of the 'access' given us by Christ. Paul goes on and lists our new privileges.

We now belong to God's people. We are 'no longer foreigners and aliens, but fellow-citizens with God's people' (Eph. 2:19). The death of Christ has made us one with God's people and we are now inextricably joined with the great body of people who have belonged to him through history.

Strange to say, although we are no longer excluded from citizenship with God's people, there is another sense whereby we are still 'foreigners and aliens'. Now we have become strangers to this world; this planet is no longer our home. As the writer to the Hebrews says, 'we do not have an enduring city, but we are looking for the city that is to come' (Heb. 13:14).

We are now members of God's family. We are more than mere citizens of a heavenly realm, because we are 'members of God's household' (Eph. 2:19). If you list the different names used of the followers of Christ in the New Testament, you will see that there is a progression. It starts with 'followers' and runs through 'disciples', 'friends', 'table companions', and ends with 'members of the family'. The reconciling work of Christ has made us children of God. We can now approach him as our Father, and a consequence of this is that no matter what colour our skin or what our ethnic group, if we are 'in Christ', then we are brothers and sisters in the same family.

We are now the building of God. We are 'built on the foundation of the apostles and prophets' (Eph. 2:20). Elsewhere Paul says that Christ is the 'foundation' (1 Cor. 3:11), but here he says that the 'apostles and prophets' are too. He is referring to that tiny band of men who spent some time with Jesus before being sent out to preach the gospel. Can you, for a moment, think of God's people as a stone building in the shape of an arch? Each stone has a function to support and be supported, and Christ is the keystone, 'the chief cornerstone' (1 Pet. 2:6–7) that holds everything together and in place.

We are now the temple of the living God. In our culture, it is much more exciting to suggest that the church is *God's family* than to say it is *his building*. But in the Old Testament the Temple wasn't merely a place of worship. Everybody knew that it was also the place where God's presence was located on earth. It is the same with the church. 'In him the whole building is joined together and rises to become a holy temple in the Lord. And in him you too are being built together to become a dwelling in which God lives by his Spirit' (Eph. 2:21–22).

One immediate implication of all this is that we should start to appreciate other Christians. All committee meetings, all social gatherings, the times we spend in church on a Sunday, should now be approached in a new way. As C. S. Lewis once remarked in Oxford, 'There are no ordinary people in the kingdom of heaven.'

Discovering the treasure

It is very obvious that we are not the people we should be. The church Paul has in mind is far beyond the experience of most of us. How do we change that?

On 6 January 1822, a poor pastor's wife in Germany gave birth to a son. She had no way of knowing that he would grow up to be a famous archaeologist and an extremely wealthy man.

Later, Heinrich Schliemann recalled that as a child his imagination was gripped by a picture which used to hang on the walls of his bedroom. It portrayed the ancient city of Troy in flames. When he left college he felt that Homer's great poems, the *Iliad* and the *Odyssey*, had some connection with historical fact and that Troy really existed. This was in spite of the fact that the popular belief of his day suggested that Troy was a fictitious city.

Eventually in 1873 he uncovered the site of Troy and a mass of treasures that made him an extremely wealthy man. He dared to believe the ancient records and acted accordingly. We start with an advantage; we know that our 'ancient records' are trustworthy. So let's dare to believe what the New Testament says and discover the 'treasure' that will be the pattern of the sort of church that Paul had in mind.

8

Oh, I forgot to say

(Ephesians 3:1–13)

We have already noticed that when Paul began this letter, the first sentence was so full of truth that ideas seemed to flow from him without any hesitation. In chapter 3 we now come to a point where he falters, pauses and seems to lose his train of thought. What we have, of course, is a digression; it begins with 'you Gentiles – ' in verse 1 and continues down to verse 13. Those who study Paul's writing are aware that when this happens, his grammar goes a little haywire, but he always manages to provide us with 'conspicuous treasures of revelation'.[1] So let's begin to discover some of the treasures here.

Let me remind you that Paul was a prisoner (Eph. 6:20). He was 'a caged eagle penned within Nero's prison bars'.[2] It's easy to sympathize with that as the cause of his distraction. He had been telling the Ephesians that as Christians they had 'every spiritual blessing in Christ' (Eph. 1:3). Perhaps in his imagination Paul could hear their reply as they saw his chains: 'How can you say that, Paul, when you haven't got everything? You're not free – you're Nero's prisoner!' Paul counters by saying that he regards himself as 'the prisoner of Christ Jesus' (Eph. 3:1). The subject on his mind is suffering, and his own in particular. That is obvious because of the end of the parenthesis, when he says, 'I ask you, therefore, not to be discouraged because of my sufferings for you' (Eph. 3:13).

God's Masterplan

The reason Paul has an insight into his situation is that he has come to understand God's Masterplan, his 'eternal purpose' (Eph. 3:11). If we were to use a technical word, as Paul does here, we would say he had come to understand the 'mystery'. He says, 'Surely you have heard about . . . God's grace that was given to me . . . that is, the mystery made known to me by revelation' (Eph. 3:2–3). We noticed earlier (Eph. 1:8–9; see page 23) that a 'mystery' isn't something puzzling or incomprehensible. It is the truth that God has chosen to reveal, which would otherwise have remained hidden. It is *revealed truth*, as distinct from the things that people can discover for themselves.

Paul has several things he wants to say about God's revelation through Christ, which he sums up as 'the mystery of Christ' (Eph. 3:4). The culmination of history is that 'the Gentiles are heirs together with Israel' (verse 6). When reading the Old Testament you could be forgiven for thinking otherwise. So often it would seem that the Hebrews were the pinnacle of God's redemptive purpose. The truth about the Gentiles (the non-Jews) was 'not made known to men in other generations' (verse 5). But now it has been revealed 'by the Spirit to God's holy apostles and prophets' (verse 5).

The Gentiles were not an afterthought

The revelation is that the Gentiles are 'heirs together with Israel, members together of one body, and

70

sharers together in the promise in Christ Jesus' (Eph. 3:6).

Imagine for a moment that your father is a farmer. He has a small piece of land which, with modern technology and your help, he can manage. But while you are away at college, you decide that teaching would fit your gifts better than working on a farm. You explain this to your father, who understands, and hires a young man to assist with the heavy work. Over the years, this young man virtually becomes a 'son' to your father. It is no surprise that when your father dies, he leaves half his land to you and the other half to the young man. You are joint heirs, but there is a difference. After all, you are the child of your father's loins; you are his son and the young man isn't.

Now that is not the position in this letter. The Hebrews are not the genuine children, with the Gentiles an afterthought. Rather, the Gentiles were 'heirs together with Israel, members together of one body, and sharers together in the promise in Christ' (Eph. 3:6). When the Gentiles were redeemed their position was no different from that of the Hebrews. That is the point Paul is making.

In spiritual terms, the Gentiles could have felt inadequate when they compared themselves with the Jews who had hundreds of years of redemptive history. Instead, they would be encouraged to know that they were the culmination of God's plan of salvation. Many in the young church would feel socially inferior to the Roman citizen who strode through life unhindered by the shackles of poverty, class or lack of education. They must have been cheered to know they were part of God's original plan and that the Roman, outside Christ, wasn't.

71

It is equally true for us. Whatever our background, education or culture, if we are 'in Christ' then God 'chose us . . . before the creation of the world' (Eph. 1:4). We are part of the original plan too.

The making of a minister

Once we have become aware of this truth, we have the responsibility of sharing it with others. This is the ministry which all Christians are called to perform. We need to become, like Paul, 'a servant of this gospel' (Eph. 3:7).

A 'minister' is someone who shares the gospel truth with others. To become a minister, it is first necessary that 'God's grace' is seen in our lives 'through the working of his power' (Eph. 3:7).

It was while Paul was still 'breathing murderous threats against the Lord's disciples' (Acts 9:1) that God met him on the road to Damascus and converted him. Whichever ministry we're going to undertake, first of all we need to be converted by the working of God's power.

Paul's view of himself as a minister is that he is 'less than the least of all God's people' (Eph. 3:8). Paul is making up words again, and once more his grammar goes adrift. He says, in effect, 'I am the leastest of all God's people.' It isn't rhetoric. When Paul looks at God's redemptive plan for the world, he sees himself as the smallest cog in the machinery that will bring this plan into being. And if God is to use us, that is how we must regard ourselves.

'The riches of Christ'

Paul makes it clear that those who minister will never be able to exhaust the 'treasury' of Christ. The 'riches of Christ' are 'unsearchable' (Eph. 3:8); they can't be mapped out. They are so vast that they cannot be traced out by human footprints. Two thirds of this planet is covered with water. If we decided to chart this water, we would have to circumscribe all the oceans, seas, rivers and lakes and then map out every bit of them from the bed to the surface, carefully recording each underwater mountain and valley. A daunting task for one lifetime.

Paul says that the 'riches of Christ' are so vast that they too are unfathomable; we will never come to the end of them.

Paul then adds 'the manifold wisdom of God' to the message that the church should make known (Eph. 3:10). If the riches of Christ are so enormous that they are beyond exploration, we now see that 'the manifold wisdom of God' is so comprehensive that there is no human condition or experience that is beyond his understanding or his ability to help.

The minister's task is to 'make plain to everyone' God's 'eternal purpose' (Eph. 3:9, 11). It is only when you explore these verses that you begin to see the privilege of ministry; that the church's message is to reach far beyond the present world, even beyond time, to declare to all people, and the hosts of heaven too, God's Masterplan.

Preaching by lip and life

Never again need we be discouraged by speaking to a tiny Christian meeting or an almost empty church in the heart of the country, because the message the minister declares will be heard by 'the rulers and authorities in the heavenly realms' (Eph. 3:10). Again, the truth here is much bigger than we might think.

Yes, our preaching is 'to make plain to everyone' (verse 9) from the hosts of heaven to the whole world, 'the manifold wisdom of God' (verse 10). But if we take the thrust of the paragraph as a whole we will see that when men and women start enjoying the 'riches of Christ' (verse 8) in their everyday lives, and when we experience 'the working of his power' (verse 7) and know the 'mystery, which for ages past was kept hidden' (verse 9), then without opening our mouths we are declaring the 'incomparable riches of his grace' (Eph. 2:7). It is God's intention 'that now, through the church' (Eph. 3:10) this should happen; that our lives should show that we have been 'made-alive-together-with Christ' and 'raised-together-with Christ'. We must learn to preach by life as well as by lip.

Paul's friends in Ephesus might be tempted to think that he hadn't obeyed God or he wouldn't be Nero's prisoner. So he reassures them that his present hardships are in fact a sign of his obedience as a servant of the gospel. If they could only appreciate that, far from being discouraged, they too would glory in his sufferings as he had learned to do because he believed God's Masterplan was being fulfilled.

9

From prison cell to prayer cell

(Ephesians 3:14–21)

There is almost a tradition that when Christians are put into prison they use the time profitably if they have the opportunity. That certainly happened in the seventeenth century, when John Bunyan's twelve years of isolation gave the world *Pilgrim's Progress*. And Dietrich Bonhoeffer's imprisonment in World War II produced his famous *Letters and Papers from Prison*. Paul used his time wisely too; he would evangelize (Phil. 1:12) or write to the churches he had established. His rough prison chamber, so to speak, frequently became a prayer cell.

Paul prays for the Ephesians

He had been writing to the Ephesians about God's 'eternal purpose' (Eph. 3:11) and the part they should play as a church in allowing his grace to be seen. Paul hoped that they would see that his present difficulties were indications of his obedience to God's plan, and that they too were part of God's 'eternal purpose' and not otherwise. This thought causes him to pray, 'For this reason I kneel before the Father (Eph. 3:14).

The normal Jewish attitude for prayer was to stand with arms slightly raised and hands open upwards, showing a readiness to receive whatever God chose to give.[1] If we had asked a slightly different question, 'Is there a special position for prayer in the Bible?', then we would have to say, 'Kneel before the Father.' On the occasion of the dedication of the Temple in the Old Testament, King Solomon got down on his knees (2 Ch. 6:13). Jesus did the same on the night before his betrayal in the Garden of Gethsemane (Lk. 22:41), as did Paul when he was saying goodbye to the Ephesian elders in the Acts of the Apostles (Acts 20:36). There is, however, no special physical position for prayer demanded in the Scriptures. We can pray just as well walking, sitting, or lying down; but somehow kneeling seems to prepare us in a way that no other attitude can.

While the Bible doesn't concern itself with the exact physical position we should take, it does presume that we will pray. Paul kneels 'before the Father, from whom his whole family in heaven and on earth derives its name' (Eph. 3:14–15). The words Paul uses for 'Father' and 'family' are closely related. He is praying to the one from whom all fatherhood comes, to the underived Father, to the one from whom every species of fatherhood in the universe ultimately has its origin.

There are well over a hundred different names for God in the Bible.[2] But they all go back to the single idea of the Creator God who has revealed himself in the Bible and in history, through his Son Jesus Christ; a God who desires to save and help those who turn to him. It is to this God that we must turn in prayer: the one whom Paul called 'Father'.

Paul's prayers are a feature of his writing and we have two notable examples in this letter. In chapter 1, the emphasis of his prayer was on the things that he wants the Ephesians to *know*: that they might know God better; know the hope to which he had called them; enjoy the riches of his glorious inheritance and know the working of his great power (Eph. 1:17–19). In this chapter the emphasis moves from *enlightenment* to a much more straightforward *enabling*. There are now things Paul wants the Ephesians to *have*. Let's notice them.

Strengthened by the Holy Spirit

Firstly, Paul wants them to be 'strengthened' with the 'the Spirit's re-inforcement' (Eph. 3:16, J. B. Phillips' translation). There is no doubt that this prayer can be fulfilled, because the answer will come from the adequacy of God's 'glorious riches' (verse 16): the riches of the one we have in mind as we pray, the one from whom all fatherhood was derived. So he won't have any difficulty in meeting the Ephesians' need.

This equipping is to take place in their 'inner being' (verse 16); that is, within their real selves. We are used to 'putting on a brave face' to the world, or to having a 'stiff upper lip' when things go wrong. But there are times when such things are inappropriate, pointless and even impossible: for instance, the moment we are put on to a hospital trolley and wheeled into the operating theatre. At that moment it is the real 'us' that needs help, not the one that we normally show to the world. When our world collapses around us – perhaps we lose our health, our financial security or someone we love – the strengthening of the Holy Spirit in our 'inner being' enables us to know by faith that Christ dwells in our hearts. It is worth noting that it is not our egos but our real selves, our inner beings, that the Holy Spirit strengthens.

'Abide with me'

That 'Christ may dwell in your hearts through faith' (Eph. 3:17) is the second request in Paul's prayer. The word 'dwell' means 'to settle down and be at home' permanently.[3]

I am never certain why, but at the Cup Final at Wembley, the crowd often sing Henry Francis Lyte's old hymn, 'Abide With Me'. One verse says:

> Not a brief glance I beg, a passing word,
> But as thou dwelt with thy disciples, Lord,
> Familiar, condescending, patient, free,
> Come, not to sojourn, but abide with me.

When we are strengthened by the Holy Spirit, Christ comes not merely to 'sojourn' but to 'abide' with us. He settles down with us permanently.

Grasping the love of Christ

Thirdly, Paul prays that the Ephesians will 'grasp . . . the love of Christ' (Eph. 3:18). 'Grasping' means both to 'apprehend' and to 'comprehend'. We are so to take hold of the idea of Christ's love that it takes hold of us and we become 'rooted and established' in it (verse 17); just like a well-planted tree or a well-founded building, because then 'nothing is able to shake' our faith.[4]

By the empowering of the Spirit and the indwelling Christ we are to move into an enjoyment of the love of Christ. It is the enjoyment of this love which is important; it is not necessary to know the specific measurements of each of the dimensions. We don't need to know in cubic metres, or the precise light years per second, 'how wide and long and high and deep' it is (Eph. 3:18). The point is that it is limitless and boundless. As one commentator puts it, we are simply 'to feel with heart and mind and intuition the "many dimensions" of love, and to work and weave that love into the fabric of life'.[5] After all, it is a paradox 'to know' what 'surpasses knowledge' (verse 19), but that is what you do with paradoxes: you enjoy them, you don't struggle to define them.

'The fulness of God'

Fourthly, the result of this enjoyment is that the Ephesians would 'be filled to the measure of all the fulness of God' (Eph. 3:19). Let Paul's imagery sink in for a moment. The first pictures that come to mind will be improbable. We might imagine something like the engine of a jumbo jet being attached to a lawnmower; or a Himalayan mountain being dumped into the garden of a small town house; or all the oceans of the world being poured into a child's bucket at the seaside.

So, what does Paul mean by the phrase, 'filled to the measure of all the fulness of God'? In the New Testament we have an example of someone who was filled with God. In Colossians we are told that in Jesus Christ 'all the fulness of the Deity lived in bodily form' (Col. 2:9). There is nothing in the New Testament to suggest that Jesus was a monster, a spiritual 'Elephant Man' with divinity attached like a gross appendage. The evidence is quite the reverse, yet in him 'the fullness of the Godhead dwelt bodily' (AV). In other words, 'the fulness of God' was seen in the life of Christ, recognizable in his character, attitudes and disposition.

So the result of Paul's prayer was that as the

Ephesians began to grasp something of the limit-lessness of Christ's love, they would be 'filled with the measure of all the fulness of God'. The life of God would once again be seen in the soul of man. Handley Moule says we have 'no fanatical rhetoric here, nor the least mingling and confusion of the finite and infinite. The idea is of a vessel connected with an abundant source external to itself, and which will be filled up to its capacity if the connection is complete.'[6] If the Ephesians need peace, it is divine peace that they will have. If they need joy, it is God's joy that they will experience.

A benediction

So Paul has prayed for the Ephesians and we would do well to echo his prayer for one another! He has prayed that they will be enabled with God's help; that they might be reinforced by the Spirit, and find that Christ dwells permanently in their hearts. The result of this is that they would start to enjoy the paradox of knowing the limitless love of Christ and having the divine attri-butes flooding their personalities. It is easy to imagine what happens at this point. The Ephesians would want to drag Paul off his knees and say to him, 'Paul, you can't pray for us like that. That is far too big a prayer to pray this side of heaven.'

But before they do that, Paul pronounces a benedic-tion that reveals a God who is so much bigger than they would ever have thought possible.

In this letter Paul has led the Ephesians in an upward journey of spiritual discovery, and with this benediction he now caps everything he has said by soaring into the air with a final majestic view of God. He is the one 'who is able to do immeasurably more than all we ask or imagine' (Eph. 3:20). And where will he do this? Not, as we might think, in the kingdom of God in the age to come, but right here and now in us who believe. It is to be 'according to his power that is at work within us' (verse 20). There is to be 'glory in the church and in Christ Jesus throughout all generations, for ever and ever! Amen' (verse 21). For the Ephesians, this meant first-century Ephesus, and for us it is the twentieth-century towns and cities where we live. Paul's letter to the Ephesians is about the church and its glory. In the chapters that remain we must discover what this means in the most practical terms.

Things to be done

(Ephesians 4:1–16)

Paul has given us *the credenda*, the things that we must believe, and now he moves on to *the agenda*, the things to be done. The letter to the Ephesians is like a personal Mount of Transfiguration; it begins and ends in the same place, described by Paul as 'this dark world' (Eph. 6:12). But in some strange way, as we go through the letter and grasp its teaching, we can be so changed that by the end we are able to cope with all the difficulties and problems of living in a spiritually hostile place.

Practical Christianity

The benediction at the end of the last chapter is the high point of Paul's teaching, with its focus on the 'able-to-do-ness' of God. Let's move away from this mountain peak and begin to take our first tentative steps down into the world that is so hostile to God and all those who seek to serve him. As we do so we must remember that his 'able-to-do-ness' continues as does 'his power that is at work within us' (Eph. 3:20). The narrowness of our understanding, the limitedness of our experience, and the faintness of our prayers cannot diminish that power. As we've discovered, we have been 'blessed . . . with every spiritual blessing in Christ' (Eph. 1:3), which includes God doing 'immeasurably more than all we ask or imagine' (Eph. 3:20).

'As a prisoner for the Lord, then, I urge you to live a life worthy of the calling you have received' (Eph. 4:1). The practical outworking of the 'able-to-do-ness' of God will be seen as we 'live a life' that is 'worthy'. Paul's words are actually much stronger. He urges the Ephesians to 'walk' in a way that is worthy of their calling. Indeed, 'walking' is to be one of the great themes of the final section of this book. We are to walk in worthiness; in 'holiness'; in 'love'; in 'light' and in 'wisdom' (Eph. 4:1; 17; 5:2, 8, 15). The NIV says that these five focal points must mark the way we live. So practical Christianity begins, as far as we're concerned, wherever we put our feet; each step should now reveal the depth of new commitment to the kingdom of God. Walking isn't too difficult; it is simply a question of putting one foot in front of the other, and then repeating the process.

Let's get moving

As we begin to move into the practical agenda, we must 'be completely humble and gentle; be patient, bearing with one another in love' (Eph. 4:2). Paul has urged the Ephesians to walk, and he now says how it is to be done. It is to be done with *complete humility*. Do you remember Paul's devastatingly honest appraisal of himself in the last chapter, when he saw himself as 'the least(est) of all God's people' (Eph. 3:8)? That is how we must regard ourselves. The older translations use the word 'lowliness', which means 'I-ness laid low'. The word 'humility' has an interesting origin. It comes from 'humus', which is decaying organic matter, and human beings aren't really much more than decaying organic matter! By the word 'humus' we normally mean the rich compost we put on our garden

– something which is not very noticeable, but is extremely fertile.

Then there must be *gentleness*, one of the qualities that marked the earthly life of Jesus Christ. He had his life under perfect control. In human terms we're not talking about self-control, because that seems to be beyond us, although we can use much more of it than we do. Paul has in mind a person who is 'God-controlled' – that is, someone on the tiller of a life which is already in the hands of God.

Patience is the third quality that must be seen in the way we live. Again I like the older word, 'long-suffering'. We talk today about people having a 'short fuse'. Paul is thinking of those who have such a 'long fuse' that their temper never gets to exploding point.

Finally, we are *to bear with one another in love*. The word for 'love' is a distinctly Christian one. It is so different from the world's understanding that, as William Barclay said, 'Christian writers had to invent a new word for it.'[1] It describes an 'unconquerable benevolence'.[2] If you wish, you could call it divine love, because elsewhere Paul says that 'God has poured out [his love] into our hearts by the Holy Spirit, whom he has given us' (Rom. 5:5). In one of his letters John refers to it as a 'foreign' love (1 Jn. 3:1), or even a love that is 'out of this world', something that is extraterrestrial. The idea of something alien invading this planet is normally the stuff of twentieth-century science fiction films. But John would argue that every step the believer takes in each new day should mean that more of the divine love invades this planet. And Paul would agree.

Unity – a high priority

Paul has reached the first main stop on the road to

practical Christian living. With what has gone before, I wonder if you can guess what it is? 'Well,' you might say, 'with the wealth of teaching in the first three chapters, our *worship* certainly must be different in future, and our *evangelism* – our *prayer life* too.' All this is very important, but you would be a million miles from what Paul has in mind. He is thinking of unity. He says, 'Make every effort to keep the unity of the Spirit through the bond of peace' (Eph. 4:3).

Why is unity so high on Paul's agenda? The answer is both simple and profound. Unity has been at the heart of all that Paul has said so far. He has been dealing with those who were 'far away' being 'brought near' (Eph. 2:13) and being made 'one' with those already redeemed (verse 14). If God's people have all been 'made alive', 'raised' and 'seated with Christ' in heavenly places, that in itself is a fundamentally unifying experience. And it is this being 'together with God and each other' that unity is all about.

It is not surprising, therefore, that Paul says, 'There is one body and one Spirit – just as you were called to one hope when you were called – one Lord, one faith, one baptism; one God and Father of all, who is over all and through all and in all' (Eph. 4:4–6).

The time in which we live provides benefits and poses problems for those looking for biblical unity. The more society becomes pluralistic, the less inclined it is to accept monolithic ideas. 'We're all in the same boat together' encourages a greater acceptance of each other. But at the same time it makes us overlook our differences, and there are differences in society that we must accept. Paul has emphasized that there is one Lord. We know from our study that this is Jesus Christ (Eph. 1:1), who was both man and God. Therefore any unity based on a denial of the divinity of Christ is not the unity that Paul is talking about. Today there must be a greater acceptance of each other among Christians of different traditions. We must not be divided by secondary issues, but at the same time we must insist that there cannot be unity with those who do not hold to the fundamentals of biblical truth. It will take time and be very painful, but we must work through this issue. Look back at verse 3: 'Make every effort . . . .' One dictionary defines the word that Paul uses here as 'to push on with something quickly, assiduously, zealously' and 'to get seriously involved'.[3] That is exactly what we must do.

Diversity of gifts

Paul moves from the unity that marks the faith of all true believers, to the diversity of gifts that they enjoy. 'To each one of us grace has been given as Christ apportioned it' (Eph. 4:7). Paul is going to talk about how these very different gifts can be used to confirm the essential unity that you would expect to find in a mature church; one that has attained 'the whole measure of the fulness of Christ' (Eph. 4:13). But he begins with the idea that every gift is essentially a gift of grace from the exalted Christ.

To make the point he quotes from a psalm, 'When he ascended on high, he led captives in his train and gave gifts to men' (Ps. 68:18). The psalm depicts a conquering king returning to Mount Zion. He ascends the steep streets of the Holy City laden with gifts and booty. At the rear of the procession he is attended by a long train of captives in chains, demonstrating his power to conquer. The psalm's message appropriately pictures Christ's victory over God's enemies. His conquest is complete and he returns to his throne in triumph. The message wouldn't be lost on the Ephesians, because, although the events of the psalm are typically Jewish, they happened in the Roman world too, when a victorious general returned home (2 Cor. 2:14).

So the exaltation of the conquering Christ is complete; he returns to his throne gathering to himself the spoils of victory, which he then showers as gifts on his church. There is an alternative reading at this point in the psalm, and Paul chooses the one that speaks of Christ 'giving' gifts to underline the point he is making.[4]

'What does "he ascended" mean except that he also descended to the lower, earthly regions? He who descended is the very one who ascended higher than all the heavens, in order to fill the whole universe' (Eph. 4:9–10). Without doubt this is the most difficult verse in the letter. Many commentators see a reference here to Christ descending to the place of the dead in fulfilment of various other Bible verses (Phil. 2:5–11), but that doesn't fit with what Psalm 68 is saying. Surely, what we have here is a contrast. The one who ascended 'higher than all the heavens' in exaltation is exactly the same one who 'descended to the lower, earthly regions' in humiliation. He is the one who became man and in degradation went to the cross for our redemption (Acts 2:25–35; Pss. 16:10; 110:1).

The spoils of victory

We now look at the gifts which the exalted Christ bestows on his church. 'It was he who gave some to be apostles, some to be prophets, some to be evangelists, and some to be pastors and teachers' (Eph. 4:11). There are three lists of gifts in the New Testament (1 Cor.

12:4–11; 27:31; Rom. 12:3–8; Eph. 4:11). For the Ephesian church's well-being, Paul sees that four different sorts of gifted people are necessary.

Apostles. We have already noticed that the word simply means 'one who is commissioned for a particular task'. Jesus had many 'disciples' but only twelve 'apostles' (Mt. 10:14). These men were his representatives who formed the foundation of the early church. It was necessary to be a personal witness of the resurrection to be a member of this group.

Prophets. Once we think of this group our minds immediately jump to those who have the ability to predict the future. But that is a very slender aspect of their work. The main Bible word speaks of those who 'did not so much foretell the future as forth-tell the will of God'.[5] The most important Old Testament word for 'prophet' pictures people who are rather like oil wells, 'gushing out' God's truth. In a church that didn't have the New Testament Scriptures, it was essential to have people who could reveal the truth for the congregation.

Evangelists. These were 'bearers of the good news'; they took the good news about Jesus to the world which hadn't heard about it. They are told 'to do the work of an evangelist' (2 Tim. 4:5), even if they don't have the gift.

Finally there were *pastors and teachers.* It would seem that this double phrase described one person,[6] the teacher who also shepherded the flock. In one sense they are the most important people in this list, because, unlike the others, they weren't wanderers. They were committed to a settled ministry in a particular place.

These gifted people were 'to prepare God's people for works of service, so that the body of Christ may be built up' (Eph. 4:12). Our view of the ministry is normally of a select few, who do the work. But that couldn't be further from Paul's mind. He sees a handful of gifted people who act as servants, a sort of 'Supply Corps' who equip the saints 'for the work of ministry' (Eph. 4:12, AV). If this was reflected in the architecture of our church buildings today, we would need to raise the congregation at the front, because theirs is the main task, with the so-called 'ministers' and other leaders sitting in a space below, emphasizing that they are merely facilitators.

I believe that, potentially, everyone has a gift that should be used. But it might take several years to determine exatly what that gift is. For a whole variety of reasons we might never be able to use our gift, and it might be wrong for us even to think of doing so. One thing that must be altered today is the expectation that every pastor-teacher is an ecclesiastical whizz-kid. There is no suggestion in the New Testament that one person should carry the burden of being a managing director, entrepreneur, super-salesman, diplomat and accountant all rolled into one.

Becoming mature

Probably the reason there are few mature fellowships and even fewer spiritually adult Christians is that we don't spend enough time studying the biblical idea of the church. The result is that 'the body of Christ' is not 'built up' as it should be. When it is, not only will the individual members be mature, but corporately the church will come of age too, and attain 'to the whole measure of the fulness of Christ' (Eph. 4:13). Then there will be a deep experience of unity, because there will be a unity of faith among believers. It will be a fact springing from a common sharing 'in the knowledge of the Son of God' (Eph. 4:13); there will be no need to 'make every effort' (Eph. 4:3).

Gone will be the childish behaviour of the nursery and the instability that used to sweep us 'here and there by every wind of teaching and by the cunning and craftiness of men' (Eph. 4:14). 'Instead' we will 'speak the truth in love', literally 'truthing it in love' (verse 15). In this context the verb means 'not only *speaking* the truth but living and acting it as well'.[7] And so 'we will in all things grow up into him who is the Head, that is, Christ' (verse 15). One writer illustrates this by pointing out that a baby's head is very large in relation to its body, and that its body, as it develops, is really growing up more and more into proportion with the head.[8] That is certainly Paul's picture of a maturing church.

If you want to know what this means in terms of relationships between church members, they will be 'joined and held together' (Eph. 4:16). They will be 'supporting ligaments' that grow and build each other 'up in love, as each part does its work' (verse 16). For a church to be healthy and efficient, every member must be integrated into the whole, and each complete his appointed task. This can happen only when Christ is truly the Head and every member moves under his control, as a healthy body responds to the instructions of the head.

Taking off the grave-clothes

(Ephesians 4:17–32)

When a church is working as it should, with each member united in the 'bond of peace' and growing 'in the knowledge of the Son of God', a new pattern of behaviour should emerge. Paul highlights the difference between the old and the new life, and urges the Ephesians to live 'no longer' as they used to (Eph. 4:17). He wants them to begin to reflect all that they have discovered in Christ.

Features of the old life

There were three features that marked their old behaviour. Firstly, a 'hardening of their hearts' (Eph. 4:18), which ultimately made them reject anything to do with God. It was a petrifying process which had slowly taken over their thinking and decision-making. Eventually they would seize up altogether. Paul's word describes a process which would conclude with their hearts being harder than stone. In a medical sense it describes the callus that forms after a bone is broken and which, once the healing is complete, would be harder than the original bone. This 'hardening' resulted in the 'ignorance' that separated them 'from the life of God' (verse 18). It starved them of divine enlightenment, which meant that they would remain 'in the futility of their thinking' (verse 17) and 'darkened in their understanding' (verse 18).

Secondly, their lives were marked by an insatiable lust that made them give 'themselves over to sensuality' (verse 19). This they did without any thought for anybody else. In normal circumstances most people would feel a little ashamed of such lust. The word used here describes those who were willing to parade it shamelessly. Their only concern was that their lust should be satisfied, and if necessary they were willing to grovel and whine in front of others until it was.

Finally, there was greed for an endless series of shameful acts. They needed to 'indulge in every kind of impurity, with a continual lust for more' (verse 19). Their depraved desire was fired by a deeper craving for a continual experience of even grosser things.

Paul is not suggesting that all the Ephesians lived totally depraved lives before their conversion. But he is saying that, to a greater or lesser degree, these three deplorable qualities lie behind all fallen nature and that must include the Ephesians. Paul saw unregenerate humanity slowly declining towards a life marked by these three qualities of godless living; in fallen humanity there was no gentle evolution towards better things.

Putting on the 'new self'

We now turn from the old life to the new and focus on Christ and all that can be enjoyed in him. If the Ephesians had received even the most rudimentary Christian teaching, they would know that 'the truth that is in Jesus' (Eph. 4:21) demanded a lifestyle that was very different from the one Paul had described.

It is quite unusual for Paul to use the name 'Jesus' by itself. When he does, he is always pointing to the historical person. So he is saying that every aspect of the crucified, risen and ascended Christ, whom they had come to 'know', had 'taught' them that there was a very different way of behaving.

One writer cleverly illustrates these verses with the account of Jesus resurrecting Lazarus from the grave.[1] In his Gospel John tells us that after the tomb had been opened, Jesus called, 'Lazarus, come out!' (Jn. 11:43). When Lazarus appeared, his hands and feet were wrapped 'in strips of linen' and he had 'a cloth around his face'. The disciples were told to help him: 'Take off the grave clothes and let him go' (verse 44).

There is no possibility, of course, that Lazarus could have helped with his own resurrection; that was entirely the work of Christ. But afterwards he seems to have been able to struggle out of the tomb and presumably, helped by the disciples, to remove the last pieces of shroud from his body and face. In the same way, our redemption is entirely the work of Christ; obviously there is nothing we can do to facilitate it. But once we hobble into the redeemed experience, we must use every bit of energy to 'put off' our 'old self, which is being corrupted by its deceitful desires', and 'put on the new self, created to be like God in true righteousness and holiness' (Eph. 4:22, 24).

Because Lazarus was human like us, he too must have been troubled by doubts. He had to remind himself of all that had just taken place and to repudiate the old human nature that had been corrupted in the grave. He had to fix his thinking on the new life that Christ had now given him. A person's clothes are what catches the eye, so Paul takes this imagery and presses the Ephesians to take off the old and to put on the new.

The mind of Christ

This would have to be achieved by the 'attitude' of their 'minds' (Eph. 4:23). Paul isn't encouraging the impossible or simply wishful thinking. For him, the mind was the centre of the personal life. He uses the phrase twenty-one times in his letters. It speaks of a person's essential, natural, rational activity. He saw the human mind as either demoralized by sin, and therefore vain, fleshly and corrupt, or being transformed by the renewing grace of God until the Christian had 'the mind of Christ' (1 Cor. 2:16). Previously, for the Ephesians, the spirit of their old nature had dominated and controlled everything they did, so now the new life must be regulated by the spirit of the new man. Paul says to the Ephesians that the focus of their thinking must be on the new life they now possessed in Christ.

If a person continually spends his or her time thinking about shameful things – and by 'continually', I mean several hours every day – in the end there is more than a possibility that he or she will act on those shameful thoughts. I am not talking about temptation, which might be entertained momentarily, or even a little longer, before being dismissed. I am imagining someone thinking about these things over a long period of time. What truly captivates the mind will in the end control the life. So Paul, because of the 'deceitful desires' of the 'old self', urges the Ephesians to 'put off' the old and 'put on' the new. And because the mind is fundamental to behaviour, he suggests they start by being 'made new in the attitude of [their] minds' (Eph. 4:23). He is saying that if they let the new life captivate their thinking, then eventually it will invade their active lives too.

I like the idea of using Lazarus to illustrate these verses, because of the marvellous picture it provides of him hobbling from the tomb. For most Christians, our life on earth will be spent hobbling into the redeemed experience. Most of us won't get much further than that. But hobbling or not, we must start enjoying all that Christ has done for us, and, to do that, we need to make it the focus of our thinking.

Things that must be rooted out

Everything that is evil must ultimately be banished if God's life is to flourish in us. But there are some things that are so pernicious, so damaging and harmful to our spiritual lives, that they must go straight away. The first is 'falsehood' (Eph. 4:25). We are to put away falsehood and learn to 'speak truthfully' to each other. Our God is truth and it is the devil who is the 'father of lies' (Jn. 8:44); so it is not surprising that we must begin here. If you look at the whole question of truth from the world's view you will see how foreign it is to God's perspective. For instance, we know that the advertised washing powder doesn't really wash things whiter, just as we know that the car we buy won't make us more attractive, or smoking more glamorous. How urgent it is that we don't succumb to falsehood like this in our thinking! If we do we are acquiescing in the falsehood of society.

If we know Christ, we must begin the revolution of changing society, and falsehood must be among the first things to go.

Secondly, we are not to 'let the sun go down while [we] are still angry' (Eph. 4:26). Paul quotes from the Psalms (the Septuagint version of Ps. 4:4) and uses a well-known proverb to underline his teaching. The word in the psalm speaks of a 'trembling' anger. It seems to mean an 'uncontrolled outburst of selfish resentment' or a 'paroxysm of personal hatred', and it is this that will 'give the devil a foothold' (Eph. 4:27). It doesn't seem to be referring to righteous anger, which is touched on in verse 26: 'In your anger do not sin.'

Phlegmatic Anglo-Saxons need to notice this truth, because they don't often get 'hot under the collar', even when they should. The social evils of our day should make us angry.

Thirdly, we 'must steal no longer, but must work, doing something useful with [our] own hands' (Eph. 4:28). Petty stealing seems to have been a problem in Paul's day, just as it is in ours. The Christian response must be that we do 'something useful' for our society; to give instead of take. Let's not forget that stealing doesn't involve only things. In the workplace thousands of hours are stolen today by people who wouldn't dream of pilfering.

In a day when we have seen the collapse of communism, we need to notice that it is human sinfulness that is often the cause of our problems, and not necessarily a political system. The world's problems have not ended! One writer says:

> Capitalism insists that man should have the right to work and do what he wishes with his earnings. Marxism insists that what he earns belongs to the community. The weakness of capitalism is that selfish man is more interested in himself than in the community and Marxism's weakness is identical. Christianity on the other hand recognizes the

responsibility of the individual to work pro-
ductively and to share unselfishly.[2]

A handful of very nasty things

Paul concludes chapter 4 with a handful of very nasty
things that really belong in the grave and should have
been buried with our old nature. First, there is 'bitterness' (verse 31), which describes something that is
'sharp', 'resentful' or even 'venomous'. We all know
people who prickle, and who are angular even before
we get near them. We are not to be like that. Then
there is 'anger'. This word has the same root as the
word in verse 26, where it is used of righteous anger,
but Paul now depicts it as an outburst of temper which
springs from personal resentfulness. Thirdly, there is
'brawling', which is loud-mouthed self-assertiveness,
and fourthly comes 'slander', when people deliber-
ately put down others with verbal abuse. And lastly
there's 'malice', which is probably the root of all these
very nasty things.

We should now live by being 'kind and compassionate to one another, forgiving each other, just as in
Christ God forgave' us (Eph. 4:32). And if we do that
we won't 'grieve the Holy Spirit of God' and we won't
'let any unwholesome talk' come out of our mouths,
'but only what is helpful for building others up' [Eph.
4:29–30).

Role-play

(Ephesians 5:1–7)

Paul was a marvellous communicator, and his powerful figures of speech immediately command our attention. But the examples that we have seen so far won't
have prepared us for what he is about to say.

Mimicking God

'Be imitators of God' (Eph. 5:1). The word Paul uses
here is our word 'mimic'. 'Copy God' is the bold
phrase of one translator.[1] If you stop and think about
trying to imitate God, you will very quickly see that
there aren't many possibilities open to us. We might
try to create something out of nothing, but I suspect
we will find it impossible. And as for upholding and
running a universe, even trying beggars belief. So
what else is there about God that we might venture to
imitate? We would certainly do well to try and copy his
love. The way most of us first experience that is
through forgiveness. Even though he said it cynically,
Heinrich Heine was stating a truth when he said, 'God
forgives – *c'est son métier*' (or, 'it's his job').[2] So we
would expect to find a forgiving love at the heart of
living 'a life of love . . . as Christ loved us'.

Again we need to notice, as we did earlier on Eph.
4:1, that three times in chapter 5 of this letter Paul
uses the word 'walk', which the NIV renders 'live'

(Eph. 5:2, 8, 15). I much prefer Paul's word, because of the direct connection that it makes between the Christian faith and the real world. I am to 'walk in love' in such a way that it actually touches the society in which I live.

God is able to forgive us completely, because our sins have been taken away by the death of Christ (Jn. 1:29), and God chooses to 'remember [them] no more' (Is. 43:25). It is this ability to 'forgive and forget' that most human beings find difficult to emulate in their dealings with others.

Immanuel Kant, the philosopher, had a servant called Lampe. Over the years Lampe embezzled large sums of money from his employer. When this fact came to light, Kant sacked him. But after Lampe's dismissal, Kant's diary entries often begin, 'Remember to forget Lampe.' Because he hadn't really forgiven him, he could never really forget him. We need to be so forgiving in our love towards others that we forget the past, instead of constantly raking it up. Choosing 'not to remember' or 'remembering to forget' is a deliberate act of the will and has nothing to do with our feelings or emotions.

The sweet savour of Christ

There is another characteristic of the love that we are to show society: it is to be sacrificial. The phrase 'a fragrant offering' (Eph. 5:2) is regularly used in the Old Testament of the offerings in the Temple. We are not to be the sort of loveless people whom C. S. Lewis once described as 'men without chests'; rather, we are to be like Christ, who 'gave himself up for us as a fragrant offering and sacrifice to God' (verse 2).

Just outside the city of Sinope, in the fourth century,

lived a Christian called Phocas. Travellers frequently passed his gate, and he would try to persuade them to come into his garden and rest, so that they could go into the city refreshed.

During the rule of the Emperor Diocletian, an order was issued that all Christians must be put to death, and high on the list was the name of Phocas of Sinope.[3] When the soldiers of the magistrate arrived at Sinope, hot and weary from a long day's travel, they needed little encouragement to turn aside into the garden of Phocas for refreshment. He asked them about their business in the area. The commanding officer said that they had come with orders from Rome to execute a local Christian called Phocas, and he went on to enquire of his whereabouts.

'I know him well,' said Phocas. 'He doesn't live far away. Why don't you and your men rest for the night, and I'll direct you to him in the morning?'

So the men retired and Phocas went out into the garden he loved. By the first light of day he had dug a hole that would take a body. At dawn he woke the Roman soldiers and told them that he was Phocas. Bishop Asterius, who tells us the story, recounts the astonishment of the men and their insistence that they could not possibly put to death a man who had been so kind to them.

'I am a Christian,' said Phocas. 'I don't fear death. It is not important to me; whereas you must fulfil your orders. You must think of yourselves and do your duty. It won't alter my love and affection for you.' So the execution took place, and the body of Phocas was gently lowered into the garden grave. What Phocas did had about it 'the aroma of Christ' (2 Cor. 2:15).

Paul's teaching on sexuality

Our television programmes and newspapers depict a world obsessed with sex, and being a Christian doesn't make us immune to temptation or the insistent demands of our own nature. Paul doesn't pull any punches when talking about our sexuality.

Firstly, he underlines the sanctity of marriage. Paul says that a monogamous heterosexual marriage is the only place where God intended our sexuality to be expressed genitally. I am often asked at student meetings about what the Bible actually permits sexually. Normally the question will be framed, 'The Bible doesn't seem to condemn *so and so*' – and a particular form of sexual activity will be named. 'Are we free to enjoy that?' I usually answer by looking at these verses in Ephesians and point out that 'sexual immorality' and 'any kind of impurity' (Eph. 5:3) are umbrella words that exclude everything outside a monogamous heterosexual relationship within marriage. Some people find the word 'greed' slightly out of place here. But it isn't; it is certainly possible to show greed in a sexual sense. Elsewhere Paul says that 'no-one should wrong his brother' (1 Thes. 4:6), and in that instance it refers to a greedy lust that takes advantage of the women within a family circle.

Secondly, Paul draws attention to the danger of lascivious conversation. He says that 'obscenity, foolish talk or coarse joking . . . are out of place' (Eph. 5:4).

Probably since the beginning of time some human beings have reacted violently towards their sexuality. George Bernard Shaw once categorized our 'two tyrannous passions: concupiscence and chastity. We become mad in pursuit of sex; we become equally mad in persecution of that pursuit.'[4] Certainly some Christians down through the centuries have failed to understand their sexuality. For one group this has meant the prohibition of sex altogether, even within marriage; or, if it is allowed, it is something extremely distasteful. For another group it has meant licence and the kicking over of the traces altogether. An illustration of the former attitude was quoted in *The Times* recently. Sylvanus Stall, a clergyman writing in the 1890s, said that after sexual intercourse, 'The male loses his appetite. Great physical changes result. The skin covering his shrunken body changes colour, his nature become irritable and resentful, and he indulges in fierce combat with his fellows.'[5]

Paul's little word 'thanksgiving' (Eph. 5:4) can help preserve the balance. If we are truly being thankful for our sexuality, we are much more likely to use it in the right way.

Thirdly, in our present society, which is permissive in spite of the dangers of Aids, we need to notice that Paul issues a solemn warning against those who are promiscuous: 'No immoral, impure or greedy person . . . has any inheritance in the kingdom of Christ and of God' (Eph. 5:5). We are told to 'let no-one deceive [us] with empty words, for because of such things God's wrath comes on those who are disobedient' (verse 6). It is the strongest warning we have had so far in Ephesians.

Today we sometimes hear the phrase, 'sexual starvation'. I am not sure that there is such a thing, but I am certain that nobody has ever been harmed by abstinence. Unlike the absolute necessity to eat, drink and breathe, lack of sexual expression isn't fatal.

No-one has died from it, or been permanently harmed in any way. To suggest otherwise is one of the big lies of the evil one.

Living under the searchlight of truth

(Ephesians 5:8–14)

One cold, wet, January day a few years ago, after a month of severe winter storms and gales, I had to go abroad to speak at a conference. When I arrived at Heathrow the latest weather front was lashing its way across the country. The plane was due to leave at midday, but it could just as well have been midnight, because swirling black clouds had enveloped the airport in a dank, gloomy darkness.

We took off on time, and climbed steeply through the turbulence to emerge a few moments later above the clouds in a blinding burst of sunlight. In contrast to the darkness on the ground we were now in a light that appeared pure and infinite. Presumably, somewhere below, the storm was still raging, but we were bathed in a light that seemed to flood and fill the immensity of space.

Children of the light

In the Bible the words 'light' and 'darkness' are, more often than not, used in a figurative sense. We read, for instance, that 'God is light and in him there is no darkness at all' (1 Jn. 1:5). John is saying that God is altogether good and that he is not tainted with evil in any way. Both John and Paul frequently use light and darkness to illustrate the difference between the new and the old way of life.

It is easy to see what Paul means when he says, 'For you were once darkness, but now you are light in the Lord' (Eph. 5:8). It's a convenient way of summarizing all that he has said so far. The Ephesians had moved from being 'dead in their transgressions and sins' to the state of having been 'saved' (Eph. 2:2, 5). So Paul now presumes they will live as Christians should; or, to take the figure of speech a step further, that they would 'live as children of light' (Eph. 5:8).

Paul then mixes his metaphors by talking about 'the fruit of the light' (verse 9). What he means by this becomes obvious, because he then specifies three different aspects of the fruit.

Goodness

'Goodness' (Eph. 5:9) is the first 'fruit of the light' which Paul mentions. The basic meaning of 'goodness' is a generosity of spirit that overflows from a kind heart. God is described in the Bible as absolutely 'good' (e.g. Ps. 34:8), but we don't find him so morally correct that he is narrow and dull; rather, he is so good that he actually litters the world with the evidence of his generosity. Fridtjof Nansen, the Norwegian explorer, described Arctic scenery in his book, *The First Crossing of Greenland*. He says:

> You know that even the loneliest and remotest areas of this little planet, untrodden by man's foot, unadorned by his hand, hold for those who respond to their strange allure, a thousand unsuspected beauties.[1]

We are not told of the Christian views of the famous fictional detective, Sherlock Holmes, but his perceptiveness brought him to the same conclusion as Fridtjof Nansen. Holding a rose in his hand, Holmes said:

> There is nothing in which deduction is so necessary as in religion. Our highest assurance of the goodness of Providence seems to me to rest in the flowers. All other things, such as our food, are really necessary for our existence. But this rose is an extra. Its smell and its colour are an embellishment of life, not a condition of it. It is only goodness which gives extras, and so I say again that we have much hope from the flowers.[2]

I wouldn't agree with Sherlock Holmes if he is saying that we see only the 'extras' of God's goodness in the flowers, but they are certainly one of the unexpected beauties of the world. Paul tells the Ephesians that if they are really 'children of light' then it will be seen in the fruit of their 'goodness', which will litter the world with evidence of its generosity.

Righteousness

A second aspect of the 'fruit of the light' is 'righteousness' (Eph. 5:9), which is behaviour that corresponds to God's ideal. Indeed, you could go as far as saying that God hates any form of spiritual life that lacks 'righteousness' (Am. 5:21–27), because he is 'righteous' (Ps. 11:7). That is not to imply that he is under a moral law himself; it is simply saying that he is the ultimate source of all righteousness.

The death of Christ has enabled human beings to

accept God's gift of 'righteousness' (Phil. 3:19). So now he expects them to reflect it, in exactly the way that the characteristics of parents can be reflected in their children.

'Righteousness' is a cumbersome word that sounds desperately old-fashioned. However, it first appeared in English hundreds of years ago as 'rightwise', which does have a contemporary ring about it. As 'children of the light', believers are expected to behave 'rightwisely'.

Truth

The third aspect of the 'fruit of the light' is 'truth', (Eph. 5:9). Truth has been defined, in a Christian sense, as 'the actual fact'.[3] God is the truth; he is the single fact behind the universe. And the Bible is truth, because it contains the facts that God has chosen to reveal to us. Paul can encourage us to 'find out what pleases the Lord' (verse 10) because there is a 'truth' that can be discovered, within the covers of the Bible – that is the most important way by which God reveals his truth to us.

The fruitless deeds of darkness

We are to 'steer clear of' (Eph. 5:11, J. B. Phillips' translation) and 'have no truck with',[4] the 'fruitless deeds of darkness'. In another place Paul contrasts the 'fruit of the Spirit' and the 'works of darkness'. We need to notice that the 'fruit' is in the singular; there is just one glorious cluster – for goodness is one and cannot be divided. The 'works', however, are manifold, numerous and diverse; they come from the 'Prince of this world' (Jn. 12:31). They are not listed because 'it is shameful even to mention what the disobedient do in

110

secret' (Eph. 5:12). But Paul is equally firm that they are 'exposed'. Indeed, it is possible for a Christian who is trying to live close to God – in the light of his goodness, righteousness and truth, to spotlight almost unwittingly the 'works of darkness'. Have you ever been in a work situation where your effort to make a decision or act according to God's way has brought tension, as others don't share your righteous ideals? What a reassurance that Paul says here that this situation is inevitable and that we have no choice but to 'walk as children of light'! 'Everything exposed by the light becomes visible, for light makes everything visible' (Eph. 5:13–14).

Normally when Paul says, 'This is why it is said' (Eph. 5:14), he is about to introduce a quotation from the Old Testament. Indeed, what follows in the NIV is set out in such a way that we are encouraged to believe that it is a quotation from the Hebrew Scriptures:

> Wake up, O sleeper,
> rise from the dead,
> and Christ will shine on you.

But there is no parallel in the Old Testament. It could be that Paul has several passages in mind (Is. 26:19; 51:17; 52:1; 60:1). If this is not so, then he has a single verse which he thinks we will know (Is. 60:1), and he jogs our memory by quoting it loosely.

In these 'days [that] are evil' (Eph. 5:16), the way to make sure that the resurrection is past for us and that we are not sleepwalking our way through life is to 'make the most of every opportunity' (verse 16). The older translation had 'redeeming the time'. But the NIV is right; Paul is not talking about the duration of

time, but rather 'critical time', the opportunities that
God brings across our path each day. 'Opportunity' is
a good word, because behind it is the idea of travelling
'towards the port'. It suggests a ship taking advantage
of the wind and the tide to arrive at its planned destination. As we live under the searchlight of truth, we
must learn to take each opportunity that God gives.

Mega-mix
(Ephesians 5:18 – 6:9)

The third person of the Trinity is the Holy Spirit. He is the executive of the Godhead and fulfils the wishes of the Father and Son. This was so at creation, through the whole of Bible history and down through the years of church history too.

The work of the Holy Spirit in a person's life begins long before he or she is aware of it; it is the Holy Spirit who draws us into the place where God can begin to work in our lives. From the new birth to the painful growth in holiness, it is the Holy Spirit who is constantly at the believer's side. So, when Paul writes about the Christian life, it would be surprising if he didn't urge us to 'be filled with the Spirit' or, literally, 'be filled in Spirit' (Eph. 5:18).

The experience of the Holy Spirit is not the preserve of an exclusive band of Christians called 'Pentecostals' or 'charismatics'. The Holy Spirit is at the heart of the Christian life, and if you take him away you immediately cease to be talking about Christianity. You will have seen that already, if you have understood all that Paul has said so far about the Holy Spirit to the Ephesians. The Ephesians were 'marked' with the 'seal' (Eph. 1:13) of the Spirit. They had 'access to the Father', and he was 'dwelling' in them by the Spirit (Eph. 2:22). He had 'strengthened' them in their 'inner being' (Eph. 3:16) and they were to 'make every effort to keep the unity of the Spirit through the bond of peace' (Eph. 4:3). These are all universal experiences to be enjoyed by every believer.

Filled with the Spirit

The contrast is between being filled with wine and being filled with the Spirit. 'Men are said to be filled with wine when completely under its influence; so they are said to be filled with the Spirit when he controls all their thoughts, feelings, words and actions.'[1] From the frequent warnings in the New Testament, we may assume that drunkenness was a problem in the early church, and Paul states firmly that over-indulgence in wine leads to 'debauchery' (5:18).

Some find this a strange contrast for Paul to make. But there is a similarity between the two experiences. On the day of Pentecost some felt that they had seen 'drunkenness' in the streets of Jerusalem. Peter refutes this and says it was the outpouring of the Holy Spirit, promised by the prophets (Acts 2).

One of the easiest ways to understand what Paul is saying is simply to parse the clause, 'be filled with the Spirit' (Eph. 5:18). The *mood* of the verb is the imperative, so this is a command to be obeyed by all Christians, just as they must seek to obey the other commands in the Bible. The *tense* of the verb is the present continuous. So we are to 'be filled with the Spirit ... and to go on being filled with the Spirit ... and to go on being filled with the Spirit'. The *subject* of the verb is plural; Paul is writing to the whole of the Ephesian church. The rest of the New Testament would underline that all believers are to be Spirit-filled; it isn't something to be experienced by a tiny minority.

Finally, the *voice* of the verb is passive. We can't initiate the 'filling'; it is God's work, not man's. Each believer is to be totally under the influence of the Spirit.

Under the influence

When people are motivated by alcohol it can be seen in the way they behave, and in the same way the effect of the Spirit is real and discernible. Paul has already touched on one consequence, which is 'unity' (Eph. 4:13), and that is certainly one of the great evidences of Spirit-filling. Elsewhere he describes the 'fruit of the Spirit' which is to be seen in the lives of individual Christians (Gal. 5:22–23). In these verses, however, he lists four far-reaching consequences which he expects to be the outcome of 'Spirit-filling' in the church.

First, there will be a fellowship of testimony as people 'speak to one another with psalms, hymns and spirituals songs' (Eph. 5:19) which will glorify God and edify people. A 'psalm' seems to be Scripture set to music; a 'hymn' words set to music that express objective truths about God; and 'songs' are more subjective, springing from the heart. 'When I feel the touch of your hand upon my life' is a 'song'; while 'Meekness and Majesty' is a 'hymn'.

The desire to 'sing and make music' is the second consequence of Spirit-filling to be seen. Since the earliest times Christians have gathered to 'Sing and make music in [their] hearts' (Eph. 5:19). Pliny the Younger, who was the Roman Governor of Bithynia, records Christians doing this in AD 112.[2] Tertullian, one of the early church theologians, says that Christians made music together in North Africa at the end of the same century.[3]

The third consequence is 'always giving thanks to God

the Father for everything, in the name of our Lord Jesus Christ' (Eph. 5:20). Notice how the whole Trinity is involved in the thanking. The Spirit-filled Christian gives thanks to the Father through the Son, 'our Lord Jesus Christ'.

The fourth and final result is that we 'submit [ourselves] to one another' (Eph. 5:21). The picture here is of mutual deference and service. It is exactly what Jesus did in the upper room at the final meal with his disciples, when he girded himself with a towel and washed their feet. The whole secret of the Christian life and ministry, and (as we will see in a moment) of marriage, has this underlying idea of *servanthood*. It is a marvellous idea, but not easy to put into practice; the key to success is that our servanthood must be inspired by our reverence for Christ.

Because of the English translation here, it is not easy to spot the results of being Spirit-filled that we have just considered. But the four participles, 'speaking', 'singing', 'thanking' and 'submitting', are there to be discovered.

Somebody might say, 'If Paul's letter to the Ephesians is a major teaching document for the whole church, why doesn't he touch on the more esoteric gifts of the Spirit such as tongues, prophecy and healing?' The answer is that spiritual gifts can be counterfeited, but holiness can't. It is not always easy to spot a spurious tongue, prophecy or word of knowledge, but you can't fool a partner in a marriage relationship. Individuals can easily deceive themselves with regard to the more spectacular gifts. But when other people are involved, if what they see doesn't add up spiritually, they can challenge it.

We now move on to see three areas of revolutionary relationships. The clear implication is that Spirit-filling, and everything else that Paul has spoken about so far, will be seen in a believer's *marriage* (Eph. 5:22–33), *family* (Eph. 6:1–4) and *place of work* (Eph. 6:5–9).

A true Christian marriage

We have already seen that 'submitting' involves 'deferential service' and that Jesus showed this at the last meal he took with his disciples. The words John uses need to be noted: 'Jesus knew that the Father had put all things under his power . . . so he got up from the meal, and took off his outer clothing, and wrapped a towel round his waist' (Jn. 13:3–4). Jesus didn't stop being the Christ by serving his disciples. Indeed it was because of all that he knew that the Father had given him, that he chose to serve them.

So when Paul says, 'Wives, submit to your husbands, as to the Lord' (Eph. 5:22), he is not asking the wife to lose anything of her womanliness, but he wants her to choose to serve for the sake of her husband and marriage. Within the context of marriage the wife is not asked to do more than the husband.

The husband is to 'love' his wife (Eph. 5:25). Love is at the heart of Western culture. TV programmes about love dominate most people's viewing, and if the soap operas reflect life at all, then the pursuit of love monopolizes most people's living too.

A novelist of today puts it like this: 'Love is the driving human force, whether it is love in the passionate sense, filial or family love or love's obverse – hate.'[4] If that is true, why is it so difficult to find an adequate definition of 'love'?

I recently reread *The Merchant of Venice*. I enjoyed the main story again, but this time I was even more fascinated by the sub-plot involving the very attractive young 'lawyer' Portia and the three young men who wanted to marry her.

Perhaps you remember that to resolve the problem, Portia put three caskets in a room, with a clue on each one. She told her three suitors that one box would contain her picture, and that she would marry the man who chose the right box.

The first into the scene is the Prince of Morocco. He liked the gold box; it suited his style. The clue was:

> Who chooses me will gain
> What many men desire.

He liked that. Imagining that it was Portia's clue to him, and knowing that there was no other man in the whole of Venice who desired her more than he did, he opened the box. But there was no picture inside; so he had lost Portia.

The second suitor was the Prince of Arragon. He liked the silver box; somehow it fitted his character. The clue on that box was:

> Who chooses me will get
> As much as he deserves.

He believed this must be Portia's clue to him; after all, there was no other man in the whole of Venice who deserved her more than he did. He opened the box, but there was no picture inside; so he too had lost her.

Everybody sighs with relief because there's now a chance for the young and handsome Bassanio. He liked the lead box and he liked its clue:

> Who chooses me must give
> and hazard all he has.

118

So Bassanio found the picture and won the hand of the lovely Portia.

What I found so fascinating was Shakespeare's understanding of love. He knew it wasn't getting what we *desire*, or even what we *deserve*, but that it involves *giving and hazarding all we have*. As Christians we understand that, of course, because we serve a God who 'so loved the world that he gave his one and only Son' (Jn. 3:16). And we follow a Christ who so loved the church that he 'gave himself up for her' (Eph. 5:25). But how did Shakespeare work it out? Paul says, 'Husbands, love your wives, just as Christ loved the church and gave himself for her.' The husband is to give and hazard all that he has for his wife. As we think through the role of husband and wife, it becomes obvious that both have a difficult task to fulfil in a marriage.

The husband is the 'head' in a marriage (Eph. 5:23). He is the source, so it is right that he should make the first move and 'love' his wife, giving and hazarding all that he has. She then steps down to 'serve' him. 'So', you may say, 'it's the wife who in the end is the doormat! Never mind the theological language you use to disguise it; that's what you're saying.'

There is a hierarchy in marriage. I believe that the husband should take the first step down in love, and then the wife takes her step in service. And thirdly, the husband takes a further step down in sacrificial love and deferential service. If he doesn't do this, then he isn't loving his wife 'as Christ loved the church' (Eph. 5:25). If there is a 'doormat' in a marriage, then the Bible would seem to imply that it is the husband's privilege to be it.

When a man and a woman marry, they discover the

119

possibility of 'the two' becoming 'one flesh'. I am committed to a synergistic view of Christian marriage: that when a husband and wife are committed to each other in mutual love and submission, they will find that the 'one flesh' is greater than the sum of the two parts. This is an added strength and offers greater potential to deal with all that life brings, both good and bad. It is a help not experienced in non-Christian marriage.

Marriage is under attack today and that includes Christian marriages. I believe that most Christians have yet to discover the full potential of all that God wants to make available to them in marriage.

Family life

'Our youth love luxury. They have bad manners, contempt for authority, disrespect for old people. They contradict their parents, chatter before company, gobble their food and tyrannise their teachers.' Hardly a reassuring quotation, until you discover that it was made by Socrates in the fifth century BC. Maybe it is the parents who are at fault, because they have failed to give their children a Christian perspective on family life. But even if that is true, children are to 'obey [their] parents' and 'honour [their] father and mother – which is the first commandment with a promise' (Eph. 6:1–2). And it is a very big promise: 'that it may go well with you and that you may enjoy long life on the earth' (verse 3). Mark Twain said, 'When I was sixteen my father didn't know anything. When I was twenty-two, I was amazed at how much he had discovered in six years.' Whoever is at fault in the tragic situation of family life today, Paul suggests that sons and daughters who have begun to grasp the teaching of his letter to the Ephesians will now see that it 'is right' to be obedient to parents in the Lord.

And, of course, the parents have a responsibility too. 'Fathers, do not exasperate your children: instead, bring them up in the training and instruction of the Lord' (Eph. 6:4).

The Christian work ethic

We are about to look at the last revolutionary relationship that results from being 'made-alive-together-with Christ' and 'filled in Spirit'. Paul has touched on marriage and the family, and he now comes to the place of work. The scene he paints, with 'slaves' and 'masters', is unfamiliar, but the situation isn't; it is still with us as 'employees' and 'employers', and in general terms the principles still hold. The employee needs to acknowledge his earthly employer, and if he doesn't happen to be a Christian, it doesn't exempt the employee from honest work. We are to work 'wholeheartedly' and not only 'when-men-can-see-it'. Paul is making up words again. The NIV renders it, 'not only to win their favour when their eye is on you' (Eph. 6:6). And employers are to remember they have a 'Master . . . in heaven, and there is no favouritism with him' (verse 9).

It is one of the amazing facts of life that treasure can come from an ordinary day's work. Johann Sebastian Bach was a teacher and organist at St Thomas's School, Leipzig. For the annual wage of £125 he trained the choir, played at services, weddings and funerals, and produced a new composition every Sunday. At the time, these were never published; just written, sung and then piled in a cupboard and dismissed from the composer's mind. Much of it was priceless music – 'Sheep may safely graze', 'Jesu, joy of man's desiring' – all piled away and forgotten, growing old and dusty.

As his daily work in Leipzig, Bach produced 265 sacred cantatas; 263 chorales; 14 larger works; 14 secular cantatas; 6 concertos; 4 overtures; 18 piano and violin concertos; 356 organ works and 162 pieces for the piano.[5]

'Othello's occupation's gone.' Those must be among the saddest words in Shakespeare. Most people continue to find life bearable while there are things to be done. It is worth noting how often the Bible refers to our daily work and attaches importance to it. So long as we still have our work, we have not lost everything. When you add recession to the technological revolution of the second half of this century, we're told that high rates of unemployment are unavoidable. Whether that is true or not doesn't matter, because millions have suffered the humiliation and degradation of not having a job. Someone has to find an answer to the problem, even if it is only training people to cope with time on their hands. Secular society doesn't appear to be prepared to do anything much. What an opportunity for the church!

15

Spiritual warfare

(Ephesians 6:10–18)

'Finally, be strong in the Lord and in his mighty power' (Eph. 6:10). There is a battle to be fought, and Paul warns against thinking that our real foes are other human beings. No matter how vile and vicious we find the Idi Amins, the Ceausescus, the Hitlers and Stalins, they are not our principle enemy. 'For our struggle is not against flesh and blood' (verse 12).

Getting the enemy into focus

Our battle is with 'the rulers and authorities, against the powers of this dark world and against the spiritual forces of evil in the heavenly realms' (Eph. 6:12). It is a spiritual war of cosmic dimensions.

Such is human perversity that for entertainment we will frighten ourselves with Frankenstein monsters of our own making. But Paul is talking here about the most real and hideous monsters, who 'rank among the highest angel-princes in the hierarchy of the heavenly places'.[1] They are part of that 'third of the stars of the sky' (Rev. 12:4) who were dislodged from heaven by the fall of the evil one. They are at the service of 'his satanic majesty';[2] the one Paul calls 'the devil'. Dr Martyn Lloyd-Jones reckoned that 'the greatest delusion perpetrated by [him] is the belief that he no longer exists'.[3]

We must resist the temptation to see this spiritual conflict as a battle of equals. It is a struggle between *good* and *evil*, but 'Satan, the Leader or Dictator of devils, is the opposite, not of God, but Michael',[4] the most senior of the angels who remain loyal to God.

We've already noticed that God's 'incomparably great power' (Eph. 1:19) is available to us in the battle and that our main opponent has been potentially rendered ineffective (Heb. 2:14), even if he continues to rage and his minions perpetuate the fight. While the final outcome of the conflict is not in doubt (1 Jn. 3:6), we must be careful not to minimize the devastating havoc that the devil can bring into our lives right up to his final capitulation, and the 'rulers and authorities', the 'powers of this dark world' and 'spiritual forces of evil' with him (Col. 2:15). So let's look a little more closely at our enemy.

In her *Autobiography*, Agatha Christie describes a trip she made in Northern Iraq where she came across evidence of the Yezidee people. She describes them as worshippers of the 'peacock angel Lucifer'.[5] That is a marvellous name because it emphasizes his strutting arrogance and that theatrical attractiveness with which he has deceived so many.

In the Bible he has many aliases. He is Satan, a word that means 'adversary' or 'opposer'. He resists everything to do with God and his people, 'making war against the saints' (Rev. 13:7, AV) and all the 'offspring of women' (Rev. 12:17, AV). He is the devil, which means 'misrepresenter, slanderer and accuser'. He is the serpent, which speaks of his power to deceive. One of the reasons I like Agatha Christie's phrase is that it makes sense of the account of humanity's fall in Genesis (Gn. 3:1–19). If the 'ancient serpent called the devil' (Rev. 12:9) approached Eve as the 'peacock angel', then part of the deception was his breathtaking attractiveness. It is just the same when he comes to us 'as an angel of light' (2 Cor. 11:14).

He is also 'the murderer (Jn. 10:10); 'the roaring lion' (1 Pet. 5:8); 'the father of lies' (Jn. 8:44); 'the tempter' (Mt. 4:3); 'the dragon' (Rev. 12:13); 'the prince of this world' (Jn. 12:31); and 'the god of this world' (2 Cor. 4:4).

One other name, not found in the Bible but worth noting, is the one used by Aurelius Augustine, a North African bishop at the end of the fourth century. Augustine called him *Simius Dei*, 'Imitator of God'. Part of the devil's technique in deception is his ability to imitate and impersonate many of the gifts God gives to his children.

The enemy's strategy

Paul nerves us for battle 'against the devil's schemes' (Eph. 6:11), and it is important that we understand his strategy. There are four basic strands to his schemes which we need to be prepared to encounter.

Physically we might have to face persecution, illness or natural catastrophy. This is dramatically illustrated in the book of Job. A violent electrical storm devastated Job's family and property and a hurricane destroyed the rest (Jb. 1:12, 18–19). Then a most astonishing array of illnesses and ailments engulfed him.

Intellectually we feel his attack in heresy and false cults. He can blind us to spiritual reality or at least make us agnostic to it.

Morally he makes us do away with absolutes, and accept sub-ethical standards. He can fan the flames of injustice and unemployment to ferment confusion. On a more personal level he weakens our resolve to resist temptation and removes our horror of sin.

Emotionally he can fill us with fear, guilt and depression so that we no longer enjoy participation in the joy of life.

I never cease to be amazed at the number of people whose lives are ruined by guilt. Recently I met a man who had been asked for a loan to pay for a child's operation. He refused, and within days saw a tiny white coffin being carried from the house of the man who had asked to borrow the money. That was forty years ago, but ever since that time his life has been embittered and crippled by guilt. Yet, as we have seen, the experience of forgiveness is at the heart of the Christian life.

It is helpful to study the temptation of Jesus (Lk. 4:1–11), because it discloses the main thrusts of the evil one which we too face when tempted. As with Christ, he tempts us to have an *unspiritual*, an *uncommitted* and an *unearthly* approach to life.

The devil's attack takes place both in 'this dark world' and in 'the heavenly realms' (Eph. 6:12), which could be translated as 'the place of spiritual reality'. The idea that the forces of evil were 'in the heavenly realms' was too much for the translators of the Authorized Version, so they spoke of 'spiritual wickedness in the high places'. But just as paradise was invaded at the beginning of time, so the attack continues to be directed at the heart of the spiritual world where God is at work. Therefore we shouldn't be surprised if we find our church fellowship or Christian Union feeling the onslaught.

The Christian's armour

As John tells us, 'the one who is in [us] is greater than [he] who is in the world' (1 Jn. 4:4), and that should be our battle cry. Satan should be taken seriously because of his immense power, but not too seriously, because he was vanquished by Christ's death on the cross and he will ultimately perish. We must, however, always keep in mind the way he works in his death throes. It is his nature to divide; to foster petty jealousies, fanning them into family feuds which in their turn develop into national or ethnic conflicts, and even end up as international wars.

Paul is writing 'in chains' (Eph. 6:20); as a prisoner, he is manacled to a Roman soldier day and night.[6] Possibly he caught himself thinking about the soldier's armour, reflecting that some of the pieces were the 'garments of vengeance' worn by the Righteous One (Is. 59:17).

'Therefore put on the full armour of God' (Eph. 6:13). It is 'God's armour', and it is not too difficult to find most of the pieces being worn by the Messiah in the Old Testament. He wears the 'breastplate of righteousness' and the 'helmet of salvation' (Is. 59:17), together with the 'belt of righteousness and sash of faithfulness' (Is. 11:5). This heavenly armour is available for us too; we are to take it and put it on; when we do, we are secure.

Homer's great hero Achilles was invincible until the day Paris discovered that his heel wasn't protected; inevitably Paris aimed his arrow at that single defence-less spot. God's armour doesn't leave us with an Achilles' heel; it is certain and complete protection which enables us to 'be strong' and 'to stand [our] ground' and 'after [we] have done everything, to stand' (Eph. 6:13). Paul is convinced of that.

The belt and the breastplate

When I did my National Service, my heavy khaki trousers wouldn't stay up without the help of the thick webbing belt provided by the army, and once that was in place other pieces of battle equipment could be secured to it. Paul sees 'truth' as fundamental for the believer. It is the first piece of armour that we must buckle around ourselves (Eph. 6:14). It is to be a foundation garment for us, as it was for the Messiah (Is. 11:5 in the Septuagint). Here, Paul isn't thinking about intellectual acceptance of the revealed truth of the Bible – that comes later with the sword of the Spirit; rather, he urges us to 'put on integrity' (NEB) as something for all to see. Truth is a transparent, practical honesty that will 'give energy, firmness, and decision' to our lives 'and relieve us from the entanglements and distractions which come from uncertainty'.[7] Loyalty and faithfulness will be seen at the same time, as they were in the Messiah's sash (Is. 11:5).

In the same way 'righteousness' is viewed in the most practical terms of holiness in our 'character and practice'.[8] As God put on 'righteousness as a breastplate and the helmet of salvation' (Is. 59:17), so must every believer, and it is to be seen as uprightness of character which is as unmistakable as a soldier's 'breastplate'.

Gospel footwear

'With your feet fitted with the readiness that comes from the gospel of peace' (Eph. 6:15). Once again the picture is taken from Isaiah, and it is one that we often sing about in Leonard Smith's song, 'How lovely on the mountains are the feet of him who brings good news.' Ancient battles were fought by foot soldiers, so it was important that they were quick on their feet. They had to be *ready* at any time, with a sword in their hand, to advance and take any land relinquished by the enemy. While some writers think that such an idea is out of place in a passage where we've been repeatedly urged to 'stand fast' (Eph. 6:13–14), one writer says that 'to stand fast is not to be stuck fast'.[9] He sees Paul suggesting that alacrity must be the mark of the believer's readiness to share the gospel with others.

It is interesting to note that the word translated 'readiness' is used elsewhere of a 'prepared foundation' (Ps. 88:15 in the Septuagint). So Paul could be saying that the 'gospel of peace' is the sure foundation on which we take our stand.

Perhaps both ideas are in Paul's mind, and he sees 'the gospel of peace' as our foundation and the message that we should be ready to share with others.

A protective shield

With the other pieces of armour we are to take the 'shield of faith' (Eph. 6:16). Paul is thinking of the man-sized body-shield that was slightly rounded on the sides to provide protection from the flanks as well as the front. At other times these shields could be linked together to form a protective wall behind which a whole company of soldiers could take cover from a hail of missiles launched by the enemy. It is this 'shield of faith' that is to be our first line of defence to blunt and 'extinguish the flaming arrows of the evil one'. Paul's language emphasizes the potentially destructive nature of the devil's onslaught, as it comes upon us with all the burning hatred and fury he can muster. Notice that 'faith' isn't simply a passive intellectual acceptance of various spiritual facts. We need to act on the message of the Bible by combining it with faith (Heb. 4:2). Nothing else can protect us apart from an active, resolute reliance upon God.

It is at times when life seems to be collapsing around us that we will need the 'shield of faith'. At such times the 'fire-tipped darts' of the evil one will come as devilish taunts: 'Does God *really* love you?' or 'Do all things *really* work together for good, for those who love God?' Only the 'shield of faith' can blunt such 'arrows' and make them fall harmlessly to the ground.

The helmet of salvation

As Paul draws toward the end of this letter, he treats us to another impossibly long sentence; he takes a deep breath and continues, 'Take the helmet of salvation' (Eph. 6:17). The verb doesn't mean 'to take up' as with a shield, but 'to receive' like a present. The enjoyment of the 'gift' of 'salvation' is to adorn the believer's life, just as the soldier's helmet enables him to go about his tasks confidently, knowing that his head is protected.

A helmeted soldier sounds quite contemporary, so again we need to notice that the picture comes from Isaiah (Is. 59:17), where we see God as the Warrior King going into battle to win salvation for his people. And he is followed by an army of ordinary men and women, who have already received the bounty of salvation from his hand. The 'helmet' is essential for our protection; with our heads covered we can rise above the 'shield of faith' to repel Satan's most ferocious attacks.

The sword of the Spirit

We live in a day when it would be easy to imagine that the Spirit's weapons are other than Paul names here. So notice we are 'to take [we have already seen that means 'to receive as a gift'] the sword of the Spirit, which is the word of God' (Eph. 6:17).

The main weapon that God has given us to wield, and the only one with which we can dismiss our spiritual assailants, is 'the word of God'. The way Jesus used the Bible during his own temptation should encourage us in this (Lk. 4:1–11). And that is what we would expect, because it had been prophesied that the Messiah would 'strike the earth with the rod of his mouth (Is. 11:4). At the end of history the same 'Word of God' will use 'the sword of his mouth' to 'strike' the nations (Rev. 19:13, 15). At the very least, this should encourage us to study our Bibles with a greater enthusiasm, so that we have this weapon to use when we need it.

'And pray in the Spirit'

The armour seems to be complete and nothing else appears to be necessary. But there is something missing, and without it the enemy could still make a devastating attack. In the end, it isn't the soldier's armour that makes him what he is, but the soldier himself. In the final analysis, the best armour and weapons in the world could prove to be a greater hindrance than help *if* the soldier is lacking in courage and determination. Therefore the Christian is to 'be strong in the Lord and in his mighty strength' (Eph. 6:10). It is to be *God's strength* that equips and steels the soldier for battle. And that is there for the asking. We need to pray 'on

131

all occasions' using 'all kinds of prayer' and 'always keep on praying' (Eph. 6:18).

Prayer 'in the Spirit' is simply prayer that he inspires and he directs. It is the opposite of the selfish craving that seems to come so naturally to us. Almost everything that we've looked at in this letter has been related to the Spirit. We are 'sealed' in the Spirit and we have 'access' to the Father in the Spirit. We have 'unity' in the Spirit and we can defend ourselves with the 'sword' of the Spirit, so it isn't really surprising that we are also to 'pray' in the Spirit.

16

Contradictions and goodbyes

(Ephesians 6:19–24)

Paul wants prayer so that 'whenever [he] opens [his] mouth' he might 'fearlessly make known' the gospel of Christ (Eph. 6:19). He will be doing it as an 'ambassador in chains' – which seems to be a contradiction in terms, because ambassadors normally have diplomatic immunity to represent their country without restraint. But Paul is an 'ambassador', and he is 'in chains'; he's bound, but he's also free; he's down in a dungeon but he's also up in glory; he's handcuffed to a guard but he's also seated with Christ in heaven (Eph. 2:6).

As we've previously noted, the tension between the *already* and the *not yet* is part of the Christian experience, so there will be contradictions in our lives too. We can be standing at the kitchen sink and at the same time be in the throne room of heaven. We can be doing the foulest job in the most awful place surrounded by evil, but at the same time be robed in the 'righteousness of Christ' (1 Cor. 1:30). In the middle of turmoil we can be at peace. We can know both the pain of life and the joy of heaven at exactly the same time.

Some people find a letter too impersonal for real communication; they need a face to whom they can talk. So Paul sends Tychicus, his 'trusty helper in the Lord' (NEB), who will tell the Ephesians 'everything' they need to know. He will 'encourage' them; literally, 'come alongside' them. It is a startling phrase, because it is also a description of the Holy Spirit's work (Jn. 14:16, 26; 15:26; 16:7). Tychicus will bring them the comfort of the Holy Spirit.

They already relished 'peace with God' and certainly should be enjoying it with each other (Eph. 1:2; 2:4, 15, 17; 4:3). But this is more than an idle greeting; Paul must be indicating either that he wants them to experience 'peace' in a deeper way, or that this document was intended to be a circular letter to the whole church.

'True to the last, as the needle to the pole, the apostle turns to Christ.'[1] Paul concludes as he began, with an invocation of 'grace' upon all who 'love our Lord Jesus Christ with an undying love' (Eph. 6:24). Where such 'love' is present, God's 'grace' can never really be absent. That was true for the Ephesians and it is true for us in whatever position we find ourselves to be.

So we have looked at a marvellous letter written by Paul to the Christians in the sports-mad, sex-mad city of Ephesus, a tiny port on the Aegean sea. And, although it was written nearly 2,000 years ago, it is surprisingly contemporary, because Ephesian society was very much like our own.

Paul's Ephesian letter contains the 'distilled essence of . . . Christ',[2] and it moves from breathtaking truth to practical application. It changes lives; it moves from theology to biography. The young John Mackay in the Highlands of Scotland in 1903 wasn't the first to find that Ephesians 'quickened' him and made him 'really alive',[3] and he won't be the last. Ephesians is about *basic Christian living*; if that is what we are looking for, we need look no further. If we haven't yet done so, now is the time to open a New Testament and read this letter.

Notes

Chapter 1: Distilled Christianity

1. John A. Mackay, *God's Order* (Nisbet & Macmillan, 1953) p. 24.
2. *Ibid.*, p. 31.
3. *Ibid.*, p. 33.
4. E. M. Blaiklock, *The Seven Churches* (Marshall, Morgan & Scott, 1951), p. 14.
5. William Barclay, *Revelation* (St Andrew Press, 1976), p. 61.
6. Stephen Motyer, *Unlock the Bible* (Scripture Union, 1990), p. 121.
7. F. F. Bruce, *The Epistle to the Ephesians* (Pickering & Inglis, 1961), p. 26.
8. Helmut Thielicke, *The Waiting Father* (James Clarke, 1960). p. 156.

Chapter 2: The A-B-C of the gospel

1. C. S. Lewis, *The Screwtape Letters* (Geoffrey Bles, 1942), p. 12.
2. C. S. Lewis, *The Last Battle* (Penguin, 1964), p. 154.
3. H. D. McDonald, *The Church and its Glory* (Henry E. Walter, 1973), p. 11.
4. C. S. Lewis, *Surprised by Joy* (Fontana, 1959), pp. 181–182.
5. William Barclay, *The All-Sufficient Christ* (SCM, 1964), p. 75.

Chapter 3: A prayer for the church

1. John Stott, *The Message of Ephesians* (IVP, 1979), p. 52.
2. Stephen Motyer, *Unlock the Bible* (Scripture Union, 1990), p. 121.

Chapter 4: The church
1. William Barclay, *The Mind of St. Paul* (Collins, 1958), p. 237.
2. John Calvin, *The Epistles of Paul to the Galatians, Ephesians, Philippians and Colossians* (Oliver & Boyd, 1965).

Chapter 5: The crooked timbers of humanity
1. *Argus Weekender*, 12 March 1988.
2. Ian Hunter, *Malcolm Muggeridge, A Life* (Hamish Hamilton, 1980).
3. Charles Wesley's hymn, 'O for a Thousand Tongues, to Sing'.

Chapter 6: On being 'Eastered' by God
1. Ivor Powell, *Matthew's Majestic Gospel* (Kregel, 1987), p. 223.
2. John Stott, *The Message of Ephesians* (IVP, 1979), p. 52.
3. D. A. Carson, *The Gospel According to John* (IVP, 1991), p. 202.

Chapter 7: The Gentiles are made heirs of God
1. Flavius Josephus. Cf. *Antiquities* XV, 11:5 and *The Wars of the Jews* V, 5:2.
2. Discovered by Clermont Ganneau, 1875.

Chapter 8: Oh, I forgot to say
1. H. C. G. Moule, *Ephesian Studies* (Hodder & Stoughton, 1900), p. 128.
2. E. K. Simpson and F. F. Bruce, *Commentary on the Epistles to the Ephesians and Colossians* (William B. Eerdmans, 1957), p. 79.

Chapter 9: From prison cell to prayer cell
1. William Barclay, *Ephesians* (St Andrew Press, 1954), p. 150.
2. Herbert F. Stevenson, *Titles of the Triune God* (Marshall, Morgan & Scott, 1955).
3. Kenneth S. Wuest, *Word Studies: Ephesians* (William B. Eerdmans, 1953), p. 88.
4. John Calvin, *The Epistles of Paul to the Galatians, Ephesians, Philippians and Colossians* (Oliver & Boyd, 1965).

5. Francis Foulkes, *The Epistle of Paul to the Ephesians* (Tyndale Press, 1963), p. 101.
6. H. C. G. Moule, *Ephesian Studies* (Hodder & Stoughton, 1900), p. 128.

Chapter 10: Things to be done

1. William Barclay, *Ephesians* (St Andrew Press, 1954), p. 164.
2. *Ibid*.
3. Gerhard Kittel, ed., *Theological Dictionary of the New Testament* (William B. Eerdmans, 1976), Vol. 7, p. 559.
4. F. F. Bruce, *The Epistle to the Ephesians* (Pickering & Inglis, 1961), p. 82.
5. William Barclay, *Ephesians* (St Andrew Press, 1954), p. 172.
6. *Ibid.*, p. 174.
7. F. F. Bruce, *The Epistle to the Ephesians* (Pickering & Inglis, 1961), p. 88.
8. R. A. Knox, *Saint Paul's Gospel* (London, 1953), p. 84.

Chapter 11: Taking off the grave-clothes

1. Warren W. Wiersbe, *Be Rich* (Victor Books, 1973), p. 107.
2. D. Stuart Briscoe, *Let's Get Moving!* (Scripture Press, 1978), p. 109.

Chapter 12: Role-play

1. The Moffatt translation (Hodder & Stoughton, 1934).
2. William Barclay, *Romans* (St Andrew Press, 1955) p. 37.
3. Paul S. Rees, *Prayer and Life's Highest* (Marshall, Morgan & Scott, 1956), p. 47.
4. Allen Andrews, *The Follies of King Edward VII* (Lexington, 1975) p. 40.
5. Ruth Gledhill, writing in *The Times*.

Chapter 13: Living under the searchlight of truth

1. Ian Barclay, *Down With Heaven* (Falcon, 1975), p. 64.
2. *Ibid*.
3. Everett F. Harrison, ed., *Dictionary of Theology* (Baker Book House, 1960), p. 533.
4. H. D. McDonald, *The Church and Its Glory* (Henry E. Walter, 1973), p. 121.

Chapter 14: Mega-mix

1. Charles Hodge, *A Commentary on Ephesians* (Banner of Truth, 1956).
2. Pliny the Younger, *Epistle to Trajan*, X, 96.
3. Tertullian, *Apology*, 39.
4. Jeanette Winterson, article in *The Times*, 26 August 1992.
5. William Barclay, *And Jesus Said* (St Andrew Press, 1970), p. 70.

Chapter 15: Spiritual warfare

1. F. F. Bruce, *The Epistle to the Ephesians* (Pickering & Inglis, 1961), p. 127.
2. Robert Mackenzie, *John Brown of Haddington* (Banner of Truth), p. 31.
3. Quoted in Wayne Detzler, *Living Words in Ephesians* (Evangelical Press, 1991), p. 122.
4. C. S. Lewis, *The Screwtape Letters* (Geoffrey Bles, 1942), p. 7.
5. Agatha Christie, *An Autobiography* (Fontana, 1991), p. 81.
6. F. F. Bruce, *The Epistle to the Ephesians* (Pickering & Inglis, 1961), p. 133.
7. R. W. Dale, *Lectures on the Epistle to the Ephesians, its Doctrine and Ethics* (Hodder & Stoughton, 1882).
8. F. F. Bruce, *The Epistle to the Ephesians* (Pickering & Inglis, 1961), p. 130.
9. H. D. McDonald, *The Church and its Glory* (Henry E. Walter, 1973), p. 160.

Chapter 16: Contradictions and goodbyes

1. Charles Hodge, *A Commentary on the Epistle to the Ephesians* (Banner of Truth, 1964; originally published in 1856).
2. John A. Mackay, *God's Order* (Nesbit & Macmillan, 1953), p. 31.
3. *Ibid.*, p. 24.

Paul's letter to the Ephesians (the NIV text)

Distilled Christianity (1:1–2)

[1]Paul, an apostle of Christ Jesus by the will of God,

To the saints in Ephesus, the faithful in Christ Jesus:

[2]Grace and peace to you from God our Father and the Lord Jesus Christ.

The ABC of the gospel (1:3–14)

[3]Praise be to the God and Father of our Lord Jesus Christ, who has blessed us in the heavenly realms with every spiritual blessing in Christ. [4]For he chose us in him before the creation of the world to be holy and blameless in his sight. In love [5]he predestined us to be adopted as his sons through Jesus Christ, in accordance with his pleasure and will – [6]to the praise of his glorious grace, which he has freely given us in the One he loves. [7]In him we have redemption through his blood, the forgiveness of sins, in accordance with the riches of God's grace [8]that he lavished on us with all wisdom and understanding. [9]And he made known to us the mystery of his will according to his good pleasure, which he purposed in Christ, [10]to be put into effect when the times will have reached their fulfilment – to bring all things in heaven and on earth together under one head, even Christ.

139

[11]In him we were also chosen, having been pre-destined according to the plan of him who works out everything in conformity with the purpose of his will, [12]in order that we, who were the first to hope in Christ, might be for the praise of his glory. [13]And you also were included in Christ when you heard the word of truth, the gospel of your salvation. Having believed, you were marked in him with a seal, the promised Holy Spirit, [14]who is a deposit guaranteeing our inheritance until the redemption of those who are God's possession – to the praise of his glory.

A prayer for the church (1:15–23)

[15]For this reason, ever since I heard about your faith in the Lord Jesus and your love for all the saints, [16]I have not stopped giving thanks for you, remembering you in my prayers. [17]I keep asking that the God of our Lord Jesus Christ, the glorious Father, may give you the Spirit of wisdom and revelation, so that you may know him better. [18]I pray also that the eyes of your heart may be enlightened in order that you may know the hope to which he has called you, the riches of his glorious inheritance in the saints, [19]and his incomparably great power for us who believe. That power is like the work-ing of his mighty strength, [20]which he exerted in Christ when he raised him from the dead and seated him at his right hand in the heavenly realms, [21]far above all rule and authority, power and dominion, and every title that can be given, not only in the present age but also in the one to come. [22]And God placed all things under his feet and appointed him to be head over everything for the church, [23]which is his body, the fulness of him who fills everything in every way.

The crooked timbers of humanity (2:1–3)

[1]As for you, you were dead in your transgressions and sins, [2]in which you used to live when you followed the ways of this world and of the ruler of the kingdom of the air, the spirit who is now at work in those who are disobedient. [3]All of us also lived among them at one time, gratifying the cravings of our sinful nature and following its desires and thoughts. Like the rest, we were by nature objects of wrath.

On being 'Eastered' by God (2:4–10)

[4]But because of his great love for us, God, who is rich in mercy, [5]made us alive with Christ even when we were dead in transgressions – it is by grace you have been saved. [6]And God raised us up with Christ and seated us with him in the heavenly realms in Christ Jesus, [7]in order that in the coming ages he might show the incomparable riches of his grace, expressed in his kindness to us in Christ Jesus. [8]For it is by grace you have been saved, through faith – and this not from yourselves, it is the gift of God – [9]not by works, so that no-one can boast. [10]For we are God's workmanship, created in Christ Jesus to do good works, which God prepared in advance for us to do.

The Gentiles are made heirs of God (2:11–22)

[11]Therefore, remember that formerly you who are Gentiles by birth and called 'uncircumcised' by those who call themselves 'the circumcision' (that done in the body by the hands of men) – [12]remember that at that time you

were separate from Christ, excluded from citizenship in Israel and foreigners to the covenants of the promise, without hope and without God in the world. [13]But how in Christ Jesus you who once were far away have been brought near through the blood of Christ.

[14]For he himself is our peace, who has made the two one and has destroyed the barrier, the dividing wall of hostility, [15]by abolishing in his flesh the law with its commandments and regulations. His purpose was to create in himself one new man out of the two, thus making peace, [16]and in this one body to reconcile both of them to God through the cross, by which he put to death their hostility. [17]He came and preached peace to you who were far away and peace to those who were near. [18]For through him we both have access to the Father by one Spirit.

[19]Consequently, you are no longer foreigners and aliens, but fellow-citizens with God's people and members of God's household, [20]built on the foundation of the apostles and prophets, with Christ Jesus himself as the chief cornerstone. [21]In him the whole building is joined together and rises to become a holy temple in the Lord. [22]And in him you too are being built together to become a dwelling in which God lives by his Spirit.

Oh, I forgot to say (3:1–13)

[1]For this reason I, Paul, the prisoner of Christ Jesus for the sake of you Gentiles –

[2]Surely you have heard about the administration of God's grace that was given to me for you, [3]that is, the mystery made known to me by revelation, as I have already written briefly. [4]In reading this, then, you will be able to understand my insight into the mystery of Christ, [5]which was not made known to men in other

generations as it has now been revealed by the Spirit to God's holy apostles and prophets. [6]This mystery is that through the gospel the Gentiles are heirs together with Israel, members together of one body, and sharers together in the promise in Christ Jesus.

[7]I became a servant of this gospel by the gift of God's grace given me through the working of his power. [8]Although I am less than the least of all God's people, this grace was given me: to preach to the Gentiles the unsearchable riches of Christ, [9]and to make plain to everyone the administration of this mystery, which for ages past was kept hidden in God, who created all things. [10]His intent was that now, through the church, the manifold wisdom of God should be made known to the rulers and authorities in the heavenly realms, [11]according to his eternal purpose which he accomplished in Christ Jesus our Lord. [12]In him and through faith in him we may approach God with freedom and confidence. [13]I ask you, therefore, not to be discouraged because of my sufferings for you, which are your glory.

From prison cell to prayer cell
(3:14–21)

[14]For this reason I kneel before the Father, [15]from whom his whole family in heaven and on earth derives its name. [16]I pray that out of his glorious riches he may strengthen you with power through his Spirit in your inner being, [17]so that Christ may dwell in your hearts through faith. And I pray that you, being rooted and established in love, [18]may have power, together with all the saints, to grasp how wide and long and high and deep is the love of Christ, [19]and to know this love that surpasses knowledge – that you may be filled to the

measure of all the fulness of God.

[20]Now to him who is able to do immeasurably more than all we ask or imagine, according to his power that is at work within us, [21]to him be glory in the church and in Christ Jesus throughout all generations, for ever and ever! Amen.

Things to be done (4:1–16)

[1]As a prisoner for the Lord, then, I urge you to live a life worthy of the calling you have received. [2]Be completely humble and gentle; be patient, bearing with one another in love. [3]Make every effort to keep the unity of the Spirit through the bond of peace. [4]There is one body and one Spirit – just as you were called to one hope when you were called – [5]one Lord, one faith, one baptism; [6]one God and Father of all, who is over all and through all and in all.

[7]But to each one of us grace has been given as Christ apportioned it. [8]This is why it says:

> 'When he ascended on high,
>   he led captives in his train
>   and gave gifts to men.'

[9](What does 'he ascended' mean except that he also descended to the lower, earthly regions? [10]He who descended is the very one who ascended higher than all the heavens, in order to fill the whole universe.) [11]It was he who gave some to be apostles, some to be prophets, some to be evangelists, and some to be pastors and teachers, [12]to prepare God's people for works of service, so that the body of Christ may be built up [13]until we all reach unity in the faith and in the knowledge of the Son of God and become mature, attaining to the

whole measure of the fulness of Christ.

^{14}Then we will no longer be infants, tossed back and forth by the waves, and blown here and there by every wind of teaching and by the cunning and craftiness of men in their deceitful scheming. ^{15}Instead, speaking the truth in love, we will in all things grow up into him who is the Head, that is, Christ. ^{16}From him the whole body, joined and held together by every supporting ligament, grows and builds itself up in love, as each part does its work.

Taking off the grave-clothes (4:17–32)

^{17}So I tell you this, and insist on it in the Lord, that you must no longer live as the Gentiles do, in the futility of their thinking. ^{18}They are darkened in their understanding and separated from the life of God because of the ignorance that is in them due to the hardening of their hearts. ^{19}Having lost all sensitivity, they have given themselves over to sensuality so as to indulge in every kind of impurity, with a continual lust for more.

^{20}You, however, did not come to know Christ that way. ^{21}Surely you heard of him and were taught in him in accordance with the truth that is in Jesus. ^{22}You were taught, with regard to your former way of life, to put off your old self, which is being corrupted by its deceitful desires; ^{23}to be made new in the attitude of your minds; ^{24}and to put on the new self, created to be like God in true righteousness and holiness.

^{25}Therefore each of you must put off falsehood and speak truthfully to his neighbour, for we are all members of one body. ^{26}'In your anger do not sin': Do not let the sun go down while you are still angry, ^{27}and do not give the devil a foothold. ^{28}He who has been stealing must steal no longer, but must work, doing something useful with his own hands, that he may have something to share with those in need.

²⁹Do not let any unwholesome talk come out of your mouths, but only what is helpful for building others up according to their needs, that it may benefit those who listen. ³⁰And do not grieve the Holy Spirit of God, with whom you were sealed for the day of redemption. ³¹Get rid of all bitterness, rage and anger, brawling and slander, along with every form of malice.

³²Be kind and compassionate to one another, forgiving each other, just as in Christ God forgave you.

Role play (5:1–7)

¹Be imitators of God, therefore, as dearly loved children ²and live a life of love, just as Christ loved us and gave himself up for us as a fragrant offering and sacrifice to God.

³But among you there must not be even a hint of sexual immorality, or of any kind of impurity, or of greed, because these are improper for God's holy people. ⁴Nor should there be obscenity, foolish talk or coarse joking, which are out of place, but rather thanksgiving. ⁵For of this you can be sure: No immoral, impure or greedy person – such a man is an idolater – has any inheritance in the kingdom of Christ and of God. ⁶Let no-one deceive you with empty words, for because of such things God's wrath comes on those who are disobedient. ⁷Therefore do not be partners with them.

Living under the searchlight of the truth (5:8–16)

⁸For you were once darkness, but now you are light in the Lord. Live as children of light ⁹(for the fruit of the

light consists in all goodness, righteousness and truth) [10]and find out what pleases the Lord. [11]Have nothing to do with the fruitless deeds of darkness, but rather expose them. [12]For it is shameful even to mention what the disobedient do in secret. [13]But everything exposed by the light becomes visible, [14]for it is light that makes everything visible. This is why it is said:

> 'Wake up, O sleeper,
> rise from the dead,
> and Christ will shine on you.'

[15]Be very careful, then, how you live – not as unwise but as wise, [16]making the most of every opportunity, because the days are evil.

Mega-mix (5:17 – 6:9)

[17]Therefore do not be foolish, but understand what the Lord's will is. [18]Do not get drunk on wine, which leads to debauchery. Instead, be filled with the Spirit. [19]Speak to one another with psalms, hymns and spiritual songs. Sing and make music in your heart to the Lord, [20]always giving thanks to God the Father for everything, in the name of our Lord Jesus Christ.

[21]Submit to one another out of reverence for Christ.

[22]Wives, submit to your husbands as to the Lord. [23]For the husband is the head of the wife as Christ is the head of the church, his body, of which he is the Saviour. [24]Now as the church submits to Christ, so also wives should submit to their husbands in everything.

[25]Husbands, love your wives, just as Christ loved the church and gave himself up for her [26]to make her holy, cleansing her by the washing with water through the

word, [27]and to present her to himself as a radiant church, without stain or wrinkle or any other blemish, but holy and blameless. [28]In this same way, husbands ought to love their wives as their own bodies. He who loves his wife loves himself. [29]After all, no-one ever hated his own body, but he feeds and cares for it, just as Christ does the church – [30]for we are members of his body. [31]'For this reason a man will leave his father and mother and be united to his wife, and the two will become one flesh.' [32]This is a profound mystery – but I am talking about Christ and the church. [33]However, each one of you also must love his wife as he loves himself, and the wife must respect her husband.

[6:1]Children, obey your parents in the Lord, for this is right. [2]'Honour your father and mother' – which is the first commandment with a promise – [3]'that it may go well with you and that you may enjoy long life on the earth.'

[4]Fathers, do not exasperate your children; instead, bring them up in the training and instruction of the Lord.

[5]Slaves, obey your earthly masters with respect and fear, and with sincerity of heart, just as you would obey Christ. [6]Obey them not only to win their favour when their eye is on you, but like slaves of Christ, doing the will of God from your heart. [7]Serve wholeheartedly, as if you were serving the Lord, not men, [8]because you know that the Lord will reward everyone for whatever good he does, whether he is slave or free.

[9]And masters, treat your slaves in the same way. Do not threaten them, since you know that he who is both their Master and yours is in heaven, and there is no favouritism with him.

Spiritual warfare (6:10–18)

[10]Finally, be strong in the Lord and in his mighty power. [11]Put on the full armour of God so that you can take your stand against the devil's schemes. [12]For our struggle is not against flesh and blood, but against the rulers, against the authorities, against the powers of this dark world and against the spiritual forces of evil in the heavenly realms. [13]Therefore put on the full armour of God, so that when the day of evil comes, you may be able to stand your ground, and after you have done everything, to stand. [14]Stand firm then, with the belt of truth buckled round your waist, with the breastplate of righteousness in place, [15]and with your feet fitted with the readiness that comes from the gospel of peace. [16]In addition to all this, take up the shield of faith, with which you can extinguish all the flaming arrows of the evil one. [17]Take the helmet of salvation and the sword of the Spirit, which is the word of God. [18]And pray in the Spirit on all occasions with all kinds of prayers and requests. With this in mind, be alert and always keep on praying for all the saints.

Contradictions and goodbyes (6:19–24)

[19]Pray also for me, that whenever I open my mouth, words may be given me so that I will fearlessly make known the mystery of the gospel, [20]for which I am an ambassador in chains. Pray that I may declare it fearlessly, as I should.

[21]Tychicus, the dear brother and faithful servant in the Lord, will tell you everything, so that you also may know how I am and what I am doing. [22]I am sending him to you for this very purpose, that you may know how we are, and that he may encourage you.

[23]Peace to the brothers, and love with faith from God the Father and the Lord Jesus Christ. [24]Grace to all who love our Lord Jesus Christ with an undying love.

Study guide

In this book Ian Barclay looks at one part of the New Testament, Paul's letter to the Ephesians, in order to draw from it lessons in basic Christian living. The aim of this study guide is to help you get to the heart of what Ian has written and challenge you to apply what you learn to your own life.

Set aside time to work through one chapter at a sitting. Begin with prayer, asking God to speak to you through what you study. Then look up the passage from Ephesians and read it through slowly and carefully. Now read through what Ian has written and go on to tackle the questions in this study guide. But please don't be limited by what we have written. Let the text spark off other questions and issues for you to think and pray about as well.

It's important not to let these studies become merely academic exercises. Guard against this by thinking through (and, if you're with others, discussing) how what you discover *works out in practice* for you. As you finish, pray once again, thanking God for what he has shown you and asking for his help in living it out.

Although the questions in this study guide have been designed primarily for use by individuals studying on their own, they can also be used by small groups of Christians meeting, perhaps for an hour or two each week, to study, discuss and pray together. When used by a group with limited time, the leader should decide beforehand which questions are most appropriate for the group to discuss during the meeting and which should perhaps be left for group members to work through by themselves or in smaller groups during the week.

Chapter 1: Distilled Christianity (pp. 7–15)

Read Ephesians 1:1–2 and chapter 1 of this book.

1 In what ways is Paul's letter to the Ephesians 'a typical letter of the time' (p. 8)?
2 What do we know about Paul and his previous contact with Christians in Ephesus?
3 What similarities are there between Ephesus and the place where you live?
4 What does Paul mean when he describes himself as an 'apostle'?
5 How does Paul describe his readers? What does he mean? How far can you identify with what he says?

Chapter 2: The A-B-C of the gospel (pp. 17–27)

Read Ephesians 1:3–14 and chapter 2 of this book.

1 What is the 'discernible thread' (p. 17) that runs through this passage? What does it actually mean? And what does it mean to you?
2 Without looking, how many of the alphabetical headings in this chapter can you remember? Which were particularly special for you? Why?
3 What does the picture of adoption tell us about our relationship with God?
4 What does the author mean by 'the tension of the *now*

and the *not yet'* (p. 20)? What examples of this can you think of in your own life?

5 What does the doctrine of predestination mean? In what ways can it 'be wrongly applied and abused' (p. 21)?

6 What does it mean to be redeemed? Why is it necessary? How does it happen?

7 What does the Bible mean by 'mystery'? What methods do you use to discover truths about God? Why do you choose these ways in particular?

8 What does 'sin' really mean? How can it be dealt with?

9 What is God up to in our world? What part are you playing in this plan?

10 What does it mean to 'be marked in [Christ] with a seal' (verse 13)? Have you experienced this? How?

Chapter 3: A prayer for the church (pp. 29–36)

Read Ephesians 1:15–23 and chapter 3 of this book.

1 How would you go about defining what a Christian is? How does what Paul says here help?

2 'Some of us are all head and no heart, while others are all heart and no head' (p. 30). How does this difference reveal itself? Which side do you tend to be on?

3 'It is only through Jesus that ... God can be fully known and approached' (p. 31). Why is this?

4 Do you have the sort of relationship with God that Paul prays for here?

5 What are you looking forward to? What do you understand by 'the hope to which [God] has called you' (verse 18)?

6 In the light of this passage, what relevance does the

resurrection of Jesus have for our lives now?

7 God's power is 'for us who believe' (verse 19). What does it mean to believe? Do you? What experience do you have of God's power?

Chapter 4: The church (pp. 37–43)

Read Ephesians 1:22–23 and chapter 4 of this book.

1 Why does Paul use the word 'church' rather than the word 'synagogue' for a meeting of God's people? What does he mean by it? Is this what *you* think of as 'church'?

2 Why does Paul describe Jesus as 'head over everything for the church' (verse 22)? What does this mean for you?

3 What does Paul use the illustration of the church as the 'body of Christ' to underline here? How is this put into practice in your church?

4 What does Paul mean by describing the church as 'the fulness [of Christ]' (verse 23)? What impact does this have on you?

5 Can you think of any ways in which you are behaving like a 'cancerous cell' in the body? How can the body be 'cured'?

Chapter 5: The crooked timbers of humanity (pp. 45–54)

Read Ephesians 2:1–3 and chapter 5 of this book.

1 What happens when we think of sin as 'a little bout of a "sickness" . . .' (p. 46)? Why is it so important to see it as it really is?

2 What is the difference between 'sin' and 'sins'? Is this distinction important? Why?

3 What are the three areas which 'add up to a walking

death'? How much are you letting these things continue to influence you?

4 In what sense have Satan, our 'old self', and death been 'destroyed'? How does this truth work out in practice for you?

5 At what point do right desires turn into wrong ones? Can you think of specific examples?

6 How does what Ian writes help you to 'come to terms with the idea that outside Christ everyone is "dead in (their) transgressions and sins"'?

7 How can a God of love display wrath? Why do people seem to have such difficulty with this question?

Chapter 6: On being 'Eastered' by God (pp. 55–61)

Read Ephesians 2:4–10 and chapter 6 of this book.

1 Can you list the four aspects of what God is like which are 'fundamental to any understanding of the God of the Bible' (p. 55)? What is distinctive about each one? In what ways have you experienced these truths?

2 According to Paul, what does 'salvation' mean? Is this how you understand what 'being saved' is all about?

3 In what senses have what Ian describes as 'resurrection, ascension and session' (p. 55) begun to take place in your life?

4 In what ways is your life an advertisement for 'all that the grace of God can do in human beings' (p. 61)?

Chapter 7: The Gentiles are made heirs of God (pp. 63–67)

Read Ephesians 2:11–22 and chapter 7 of this book.

1 What pictures does Paul use to illustrate what Christ has done for us (p. 64)?

2 What privileges do we have as a result of what Christ has done for us?

3 What implication does Ian draw out from this list of privileges? How do you put this into practice?

Chapter 8: Oh, I forgot to say (pp. 69–74)

Read Ephesians 3:1–13 and chapter 8 of this book.

1 How would you answer someone who suggested that, in the light of his imprisonment, Paul's talk of possessing 'every spiritual blessing in Christ' is just a pipe-dream?

2 What is 'God's Masterplan' (p. 70)? How does it involve you?

3 How can we be sure that God's inclusion of Gentiles among his people is not just an afterthought?

4 What does it mean for you to be a 'servant of this gospel' (verse 7; p. 72)?

5 What is required before a person can become a 'minister'?

6 Ian speaks of 'preaching by lip and life' (p. 73). Why is this? How do you go about doing this?

7 What hardships are you facing which 'are in fact a sign of [your] obedience as a servant of the gospel' (p. 74)?

Chapter 9: From prison cell to prayer cell (pp. 75–81)

Read Ephesians 3:14–19 and chapter 9 of this book.

1 What do you think about kneeling to pray? Why?

2 Why does Paul concentrate on praying for the 'inner being' of his readers? What does he mean?

3 Does Christ 'abide with' you? What does this mean? What effects does his presence in our lives bring about?

4 What does it mean to 'grasp . . . the love of Christ' (verse 18; p. 78)? Why is this so important?

5 Ian suggests several pictures to hint at what it means to be 'filled to the measure of all the fulness of God' (verse 19; p. 79). Use your imagination and see whether you can come up with any other illustrations of this truth.

6 How is it possible for God actually to answer such a big prayer as this? Begin to let Paul's perspectives guide you in the way you pray for yourself and for others.

Chapter 10: Things to be done (pp. 83–91)

Read Ephesians 4:1–16 and chapter 10 of this book.

1 What is the 'practical outworking of the "able-to-do-ness" of God' (p. 83)?

2 What four characteristics of the Christian life does Paul go on to mention? What does each of these mean for you?

3 Why is Christian unity such a high priority for Paul? How important is it for you? Why?

4 How do you decide whether a particular difference of view is 'primary' (leading to the impossibility of unity) or 'secondary' (leading to the necessity of unity)?

5 What does Paul's quotation from Psalm 68 serve to underline about Jesus?

6 What 'four different sorts' (p. 108) of gifted individuals does the church need for its well-being? How are these represented in your church?

7 'Our view of the ministry is normally . . .' what (p. 90)? What should it be? How does this work out in your church?

8 What are the characteristics of a 'mature' church?

How does your contribution to the church help (or hinder!) this process?

Chapter 11: Taking off the grave-clothes (pp. 93–99)

Read Ephesians 4:17–32 and chapter 11 of this book.

1 What are the 'three features' (pp. 93–94) which mark the life of people before they become Christians? To what extent were these true of you?
2 What parallels are there between the raising of Lazarus and a person who is beginning the Christian life?
3 What sort of things do you need to 'put off' and 'put on'? What examples does Paul give here? How do they apply to you?

Chapter 12: Role-play (pp. 101–106)

Read Ephesians 5:1–7 and chapter 12 of this book.

1 What does Paul mean by telling his readers to 'be imitators of God' (verse 1)? What specific examples does he draw out? How do they apply to you at the moment?
2 How does Paul's ban on 'sexual immorality, and any kind of impurity' (verse 3) strike you?
3 What advice does Paul give here which will help to give us a balanced view of sexuality?
4 What 'big lie of the Evil One' (p. 106) does Ian draw attention to here? To what extent have you been taken in by it?

Chapter 13: Living under the searchlight of truth (pp. 107–112)

Read Ephesians 5:7–14 and chapter 13 of this book.

1 How is verse 8 'a convenient way of summarizing all

that [Paul] has said so far' (p. 108)?

2 What 'three different aspects' (p. 108) of the fruit of light does Paul mention? What do these mean?

3 How do you go about finding out what pleases the Lord (verse 10)?

4 How are we to 'expose' the deeds of darkness (verse 11)? What does this mean in practice for you?

5 What particular opportunities for living as a child of the light have you had recently? How did you use them?

Chapter 14: Mega-mix (pp. 113–122)

Read Ephesians 5:18 – 6:9 and chapter 14 of this book.

1 What does the Holy Spirit do? In what sense is he 'at the heart of the Christian life' (p. 113)?

2 What are a) the similarities and b) the differences between being under the influence of alcohol and being filled with the Holy Spirit?

3 What effects of the Holy Spirit's influence does Paul focus on here? How evident are they in your life?

4 What does Ian mean by saying that '. . . spiritual gifts can be counterfeited, but holiness can't' (p. 116)? How is this relevant for you?

5 Do you think that there is any difference between a wife submitting to her husband (verse 22) and a husband loving his wife (verse 25)? Why?

6 What do you think of Shakespeare's definition of love? How does it measure up to what the Bible teaches?

7 In marriage, does God intend one partner to be the other's doormat'? If so, which? Why?

8 What instructions for family life does Paul give here? How far are you putting them into practice?

9 What can employers and employees learn from what Paul says here?

10 How important is work to you? In what ways could your church take up the challenge of unemployment in your locality?

Chapter 15: Spiritual warfare
(pp. 123–132)

Read Ephesians 6:10–18 and chapter 15 of this book.

1 What does Ian suggest is the the greatest delusion perpetrated by the devil? What evidence of such deception are you aware of?

2 If, as Paul has already stated, God's 'incomparably great power' is available to us, why must we 'be careful not to minimize the devastating havoc that the devil can bring into our lives . . .' (p. 124)?

3 What are the 'four basic strands' in the devil's strategy? Which ones does he use on you?

4 Look at Luke 4:1–11. What lessons can we learn from the way Jesus faced temptation?

5 What does putting on the armour of God actually entail? As you consider each piece, think about what it means in practice for you.

6 Why does Paul end this list with the instruction to 'pray in the Spirit . . .' (verse 18)?

Chapter 16: Contradictions and goodbyes
(pp. 133–134)

Read Ephesians 6:19–23 and chapter 16 of this book.

1 Paul uses the contradictory term 'ambassador in chains' (verse 20) to describe himself. What similar sorts of contradiction do you face? Why?

2 What is distinctive about the ministry of Tychicus? Who serves as a 'Tychicus' in your life? Are you a 'Tychicus' to someone else?